Teaching Equality

Teaching Equality

Black Schools in the Age of Jim Crow

ADAM FAIRCLOUGH

Mercer University Lamar Memorial Lectures
No. 43

The University of Georgia Press
Athens and London

© 2001 by the University of Georgia Press
Athens, Georgia 30602
All rights reserved
Designed by Sandra Strother Hudson
Set in Cycles by G&S Typesetters, Inc.
Printed and bound by Maple-Vail
The paper in this book meets the guidelines for
permanence and durability of the Committee on
Production Guidelines for Book Longevity of the
Council on Library Resources.

Printed in the United States of America
05 04 03 02 01 C 5 4 3 2 1

Library of Congress Cataloging-in-Publication Data
Fairclough, Adam.
Teaching equality : Black schools in the age of Jim
Crow / Adam Fairclough.
    p.   cm. — (Mercer University Lamar memorial
lectures ; no. 43)
Includes bibliographical references and index.
ISBN 0-8203-2272-5 (alk. paper)
1. Afro-Americans—Education.   2. Segregation
in education—United States.   3. Afro-American
educators—Biography.   I. Title.   II. Series.
LC2741 .F35 2001
371.829′96073—dc21   00-045131

British Library Cataloging-in-Publication Data available

Contents

Foreword

This past fall Mercer University was fortunate to have as its forty-third annual Lamar Lecturer Adam Fairclough, chair of American History at the University of East Anglia. Born and trained in England, Fairclough has emerged as one of the brightest and most prolific historians of the U.S. Civil Rights movement. His work lends credence to the claim of one of my former professors, who has stated—on more than one occasion—that some of the best work in southern history comes from "interlopers."

Fairclough's lectures highlight the contested position of black educators in the post-Reconstruction South, both in the estimation of contemporary "race leaders" and, more recently, in civil rights historiography. Those who championed the work of black educators argued that they and their institutions sustained hope, advanced the individual, and even liberated the race. Detractors, however, noted that the optimism and confidence put in black education seemed misplaced. Education could not, they argued, liberate, uplift, or guide the race. Moreover, the conservative "accommodationist" approach taken by many of these black educators had real costs. The appeasement of white benefactors and philanthropists did little to end racial oppression. How, then, are we to evaluate black educators? Professor Fairclough urges us to abandon the stultifying debate between "race savior" and "race traitor" and consider black educators as "double agents." Borrowing from the "methodology" of the CIA and MI-5, Fairclough assesses black educators in terms of profits and losses, weighing the known goods against the suspected losses. Tuskegee, and institutes like it, provided important educational opportunities for African Americans, albeit within the context of a Jim Crow South. They gave students the intellectual space to develop a critique of white supremacy, the social space to challenge authority, and an environment that fostered the organizations that sought to dismantle Jim Crow segregation. When civil rights activists directly challenged pervasive institutional racism, however, they set their sights on black college presidents, who found it increasingly unfashionable to defend black colleges. Black educators came under attack for punishing civil rights activists on their campuses. Fairclough asks if their desire to save black colleges was worthy of condemnation, however. He suggests instead that the passage of time might make us more sympathetic to the claim that the work of black college presidents was as valuable as the work of civil rights activists.

The Lamar Committee thanks Professor Fairclough for offering these challenging and provocative lectures. The committee also thanks the family of the late Eugenia Blount Lamar, whose generous bequest makes this lecture series possible. I wish to thank the members of the committee, all of whom have made my work at Mercer eminently enjoyable: Mrs. R. Lanier Anderson III, Michael Cass, Fred Hobson, Hubert McAlexander, Wayne Mixon, Karen Orchard, John Thomas Scott, and George Tindall.

Sarah E. Gardner,
for the Lamar Memorial Lecture Committee

Preface

I am extremely grateful to the Lamar Memorial Lectures Committee for inviting me to present the ideas contained in these pages. It is, of course, a great honor to give the Lamar Lectures, and an honor felt especially keenly by a British scholar of the American South. During my visit to Mercer University, the members of the committee made my stay in Macon a real pleasure, showing me great kindness and friendliness. I am particularly indebted to Professor Michael Cass and Lynn Stovall Cass for their unstinting hospitality. (Mike Cass, I should add, helpfully and considerately rearranged the date of the lectures so as to accommodate the birth of my son, Arthur.) Andrew Manis, Tom Scott, and Sarah Gardner introduced each lecture with great eloquence and skill, summarizing their themes far more clearly and succinctly than I could possibly express them. The late Eugenia Dorothy Blount Lamar, of course, made this book possible, and I was pleased to be able to acknowledge her act of creative generosity in the presence of members of the Lamar family.

I began the research upon which these lectures are based during a fellowship at the National Humanities Center in 1994–95. The staff of that splendid institution enabled me to get a flying start on a new project by offering an inspiring combination of professional assistance and relaxed conviviality. Only former fellows will understand how much I owe to the NHC. I have also received support for this research, which I gratefully acknowledge, from my former employer, the University of Leeds, and from that perennially generous institution, the British Academy. I have been fortunate in having had opportunities to try out some of these ideas before friendly audiences at the University of Texas, Vanderbilt University, and Cambridge University. Thank you Dave Bowman, David Carlton, and Tony Badger. As always, Mary Ellen Curtin, my wife and fellow historian, has helped me to develop and hone my ideas about southern and African American history.

I am delighted that the University of Georgia Press, which has published all my previous books, is also publishing this one. I have worked with Karen Orchard, the Press's director, for over fifteen years now, and I could not have hoped for a more efficient and sympathetic editor. To Karen, editor and friend, I dedicate this volume.

1 *Liberation or Collaboration?*

Black Teachers in the
Era of White Supremacy

In 1887 Annie Day, a teacher in Beaufort, South Carolina, wrote that "my heart, as does the heart of every learned person, yearns for the dawn of a happier civilization. And I am using all my effort to instill a like longing and hope in the hearts of my pupils." In the same year, Charles Hunter, a teacher in Goldsboro, North Carolina, was enjoined by a friend to "battle not only against ignorance and moral evils but against spiritual darkness. Do above all things try to impress upon your scholars characters of truth [and] of sincerity." A few months later, in Selma, Alabama, the Reverend George M. Elliott reminded an audience of teachers that "you are the shapers of thought and the molders of sentiment, not of this age and of this generation alone, but of ages and generations to come. You are making history by those you teach. . . . You are the few that are molding the masses." [1]

My subject in these lectures is the role of African American educators in shaping the black struggle for equality. The history of black southerners can scarcely be comprehended without studying the teachers who symbolized, articulated, and furthered their aspirations. Lucy Laney, Richard R. Wright, John Hope, Charlotte Hawkins Brown, Mary McLeod Bethune, and a small army of now-forgotten pioneers shared a missionary fervor about the value of education that profoundly influenced millions of black Americans. Teachers also played a wider role in the black community. Education has been one of the most important political battlefields in the South, and black teachers were at the center of that battlefield. [2] Southern whites sought to control them, fearful that educated blacks would lead movements for equality. Many whites opposed black education altogether. Education not only pitted blacks against whites but also aroused passionate debates among blacks themselves. Booker T. Washington, who founded a black school in Tuskegee, Alabama, was the single most influential black leader between 1895 and 1915; his ideas about education, however, were fiercely contested by many blacks. Education polarized opinions within the black community more than any other issue: it raised philosophical questions about the meaning of freedom and equality as well as very practical questions about how to secure schools and what to teach.

My definition of "teacher" is broad: anyone engaged in formal education, whether they taught in a state-supported school or a private institution, in a creaking wooden shack in the Alabama Black Belt or in a Gothic brick tower at Fisk University. My historical canvas—a large one that requires broad brush strokes—is the hundred years from the Civil War to the Civil Rights movement.[3]

The story of black schools in the South paralleled in many ways the broader educational history of the times. The rhetoric of black teachers bristled with the moral zeal of nineteenth-century pedagogy. Members of a small middle class that sociologist E. Franklin Frazier dubbed "Black Puritans," they believed, along with their abolitionist mentors, that education was as much about industry, piety and morality as about the three "Rs." Black teachers embraced the cause of public education with all the passion of the Massachusetts schoolmarms who, imbued with the philosophy of Horace Mann, traveled to the Union-occupied South with the aim of dispelling ignorance, immorality, and superstition among a benighted race— and of establishing beyond doubt the superiority of free labor. When black teachers met to discuss education, it was impossible to infer from the titles of their speeches that they were meeting in Selma, Alabama, rather than Boston, Massachusetts, or, for that matter, London, England: "The Teacher's Moral Influence," "The Necessity of Temperance Instruction," "The Place of the Bible in Our Public

Schools," "The Attitude of Romanism to our Public Schools," "The Advantage of Beautifying the Home," "Arnold of Rugby," and "How Shall We Protect Our Girls?"[4]

In the field of education, like so much else in the history of the South, black and white were inextricably linked. The enduring influence of northern missionaries is common knowledge; less well-known is the fact that education for blacks was a biracial movement that depended upon the support of southern whites. As James D. Anderson has stressed, while there were always whites who opposed black education in principle, the white ruling class recognized the inevitability, if not the desirability, of some level of schooling for black people. The public school crusade of the late nineteenth and early twentieth centuries was slow to include blacks, but include them it eventually did. In addition, northern philanthropic foundations like the Slater Fund, the General Education Board, and the Rosenwald Fund helped to finance and shape black education in the South. Unlike the history of the black church, therefore, the history of black schools in the South was not one of African American autonomy—far from it.

Nevertheless, slavery and racial segregation meant that white southerners and black southerners perceived and experienced education in profoundly different ways. The efforts of the slave regime to prevent black literacy meant that blacks early on associated education with liberation. It is an error, therefore, to depict the African American desire for schooling—often mocked by white southerners as devoid of real understanding—as unthinking imitation of white culture. The freedmen did not need New England missionaries to teach them the value of literacy: they knew its importance already. Indeed, by 1860 black southerners had attained a degree of literacy remarkable under the circumstances. According to one historian, "Northerners were frequently amazed at the number" of blacks who had already acquired a knowledge of letters under slavery. Some of them were autodidacts; a few had learned at clandestine schools;

most had probably been taught by the very families who owned them. As much as 10 percent of the black population may have been literate.[5]

Emancipation released a flood of impatient enthusiasm for schooling that summoned forth black initiative as well as white charity. Northern-educated blacks like John Oliver, Thomas DeSaille Tucker, and John Wesley Cromwell began teaching in the missionary schools of Union-occupied Virginia as early as 1862. Clement Robinson, a graduate of Lincoln University, founded Virginia's first "normal school" for the training of black teachers in the same year. In Savannah, no sooner was the city liberated than blacks formed the Savannah Education Association, which swiftly raised $800 and founded several schools. "It is wholly their own," noted a white minister. "The officers of the Assoc. are all colored men. The teachers are all colored." In rural areas, black people organized countless "freedmen's schools" and "Sunday schools" independently of the northern missionary societies. By 1869, black teachers in the South outnumbered northern missionaries. As James Anderson suggests, the freedmen's passion for education was as much a product of slavery as a cultural import from New England.[6]

The history of slavery and emancipation also shaped the role of black teachers. Like ministers, teachers became quasi-political leaders; but because they lacked the independence of ministers, their role was rather more complex. Mass illiteracy among the freedmen made teachers a vital source of political leadership during Reconstruction. When black men gained the vote, teacher-politicians like Thomas W. Cardozo, Jonathan C. Gibbs, and James Walker Hood rose high in the ranks of the Republican party. Even after the final collapse of Reconstruction in 1877, teachers continued to be embroiled in party politics. Some, like Ezekiel E. Smith of North Carolina and Richard R. Wright of Georgia, held important federal patronage jobs. Teachers in the New South regarded education and politics as inextricably woven; they formed state associations that quizzed political candidates, lobbied state legislatures, and took stands on controversial issues like the convict lease system.[7]

Black teachers retained a good deal of influence even after disfranchisement removed them from politics, and even after decades of public schooling ended their near monopoly of literacy. This was partly because teaching still attracted black people of ability and learning in disproportionately high numbers. Racial discrimination restricted economic opportunities so severely that the occupations of preaching and teaching accounted for the overwhelming mass of the black middle class. In 1910 over half of all black college graduates became teachers, one-sixth preachers. Thirty years later the U.S. Census, surveying the number of black professionals, counted 1,000 lawyers, 3,500 medical doctors, 17,000 ministers, and 63,000 schoolteachers.[8]

Teachers continued to act as community leaders. The raising of schools was a collective endeavor that was almost as instrumental in the formation of black communities as the founding of churches. Most schools began life as private initiatives, founded on the faith and vision of individual teachers. Churches then provided buildings, farmers land, parents money and labor. Even when they received private philanthropy and state funding, black schools still depended upon voluntary contributions by patrons and heroic efforts by teachers. The 5,000 Rosenwald schools erected in the South between 1917 and 1932 could not have been built without an enormous community effort. The money allocated by the Julius Rosenwald Fund itself constituted "less than the total raised by the Negroes themselves in small amounts, county by county and village by village."[9]

Given the huge material and human investment involved in obtaining schools, black southerners prided them. Schools functioned as community centers, nondenominational meeting places where Baptists and Methodists could feel comfortable together. In the 1920s and '30s they housed adult education classes in health, homemaking, agriculture, and literacy.[10] In many rural communities, the annual "School Closing" or "Commencement" exercise was the most important social event of the year. Writing shortly before his death in 1931, North Carolina teacher Charles Hunter recalled:

> For weeks before, in every home, mothers and fathers were kept on their toes in preparation for this coming glory in the school life of their children. With the children it was one great thrill. They all wanted to have a part in the Exhibition and Concert. They wanted to speak their pieces. They wanted to sing their songs. They wanted to say their dialogues. They wanted a part in the beautiful drills. O, it was a joyous prospect, and the teachers, too, were no less moved. We were kept busy afternoons and nights in rehearsals. The work was not irksome. No one tires of it. When the eventful night rolled around . . . [t]he people of East Raleigh and of the entire city turned out. . . . The memory of those bright and beautiful days is as refreshing breezes, founts of cooling waters, invigorating elixirs, life anew.

Hunter may be excused his rose-tinted spectacles. His memory poignantly captured the enthusiasm and idealism of those celebrations. As historian James Leloudis suggests, "Through the commencement exercises . . . black celebrants found a public voice for making moral and political claims on the rest of society. 'This,' they seemed to exclaim, 'is how the world should be.' "[11]

School closing exercises were also about cultivating the support of the black community. Here was another facet of the teacher's role: schools received such paltry sums from public taxation that teachers were virtually compelled to seek community assistance. That meant, first, getting on the right side of ministers. At a meeting in 1938, Tennessee teachers were advised, "Do not fight faiths" and, above all, "Do not discuss [the] preacher's ability." Second, winning and maintaining public support meant visiting parents, and scattered evidence suggests that black teachers did this far more often than white teachers. During home visits, especially in rural areas, parents often sought the teacher's help in carrying out tasks that required literacy: teaching Sunday school, filling out orders to Sears and Roebuck, writing letters, and figuring up weekly wages. Recalled Dorothy Robinson, a teacher in east Texas in the early 1930s, "It never occurred to me to refuse their varied requests. . . . I became not merely the children's teacher but also the community's, and everyone referred to me as 'our teacher.'"[12]

The greater the claims upon the teacher from the community, the more the teacher could ask of the community. In the 1930s anthropologist Hortense Powdermaker was astonished by the indefatigable fundraising activities of the parent-teacher associations of Sunflower County, Mississippi. "Some sell chickens and eggs and put the proceeds into a special fund for the school. They give entertainments, charging five cents admission. They co-operate in renting a piece of land on which they make a crop of cotton for the benefit of the school. . . . When money is especially scarce, the patrons bring food to the teachers or board them for free." PTAs bought fuel, procured supplies, paid for repairs, supplemented the teacher's wage to extend the school term, and even purchased school buses.[13]

A desire for what we now call "community control" was a further reason why teachers played a wider role in the life of the black community than their white counterparts. As a white official noted in the early days of Reconstruction, the freedmen "have a natural praiseworthy pride in keeping their educational institutions in their own hands. . . . What they demand is assistance without control."[14] This demand often manifested itself in a preference for black teachers. Even before the Civil War ended, the American Missionary Association was taken aback when, entering Savannah upon the heels of General Sherman, its offer of northern white teachers was spurned by resident blacks. Although the northern missionaries constantly complained about the incompetence of black teachers, the latter argued that even the best-intentioned whites found it difficult to accept blacks as equals, and frequently betrayed "exhibitions of prejudice." In letters from across the South, the Freedmen's Bureau heard similar reports: "They want a colored teacher."

To some extent the desire for black teachers mirrored the preference for black ministers—it was an expression of racial pride, cultural difference, and group solidarity. Writing in 1879, Joseph C. Price recorded in his diary how he felt about an acquaintance who wished to teach in Africa. "It pleases me to see or hear this spirit in young Americans of African descent. The future educators of the blacks both in America and Africa *are the blacks.*" Price was no black nationalist, and he disagreed with the notion that black Americans should return en masse to Africa. However, as a bishop in the AME Zion Church, a black denomination, and president of Livingstone College, where blacks comprised the faculty as well as the student body, he personified a widespread belief in black autonomy and self-help.[15]

The question of black teachers was never a settled issue. Given the choice, most black people would probably have preferred a fully integrated public school system. Integration never got off the ground, however, and racial segregation became the organizing principle of the New South. In this context, more and more blacks saw economic, cultural, and educational advantages in racial solidarity. The desire for black teachers was accentuated when, as in Richmond and Charleston, southern-born whites were engaged to teach in black public schools. Such people, argued John W. Cromwell, were too imbued with the "false and wicked ideas" bred by slavery to safely instruct black children. In addition, of course, white teachers held jobs that blacks coveted. After Reconstruction, blacks pushed hard to have white teachers removed and replaced. By 1919, when the City of Charleston finally capitulated, the campaign for black teachers had triumphed throughout the South.[16]

Other emotions and beliefs fed the desire for autonomy. One was a resigned recognition of white racism and a yearning for security within the group. W. T. B. Williams, a native of Virginia who studied at Harvard before devoting his life to teaching in the South, explained this yearning to a nephew who felt isolated and disoriented living in the North: "[Your present loneliness] will help you to appreciate . . . how much you really think of colored people. Having been among them and of them all your days, you have not had a chance to know how much your people really mean to you. Blood is thicker than water. And especially here in America where race lines are being drawn so sharply as far as Negroes are concerned, colored people are very dear and necessarily near to one another."[17]

Freedom from white control had another purpose. Black teachers had something to prove: it was up to them to establish beyond question that black people could do as well as whites. Much of Booker T. Washington's prestige among blacks—in Africa as well as in America—derived from his insistence that Tuskegee Institute should be staffed entirely by blacks, showing their competence to manage a complex institution. In building a successful black college, Washington made a statement about racial equality that was far more powerful than words. "Tuskegee alone is the fruit of a black man's heart and brain and effort and administrative skill," wrote Roscoe Conkling Bruce, one of its teachers. "Tuskegee Institute is . . . irrefragable proof of the black man's capacity for the tasks of civilization."[18]

Here we arrive at possibly the most important reason why black teachers attained such an important position of leadership within the black community: they personified the belief that education meant liberation. Black southerners subscribed, perhaps more fervently than any other group, to the ideology of the public school advocates that education was democracy's great equalizer. Laboring under a double burden of poverty and discrimination, they expected education to serve double duty as a means of advancing both the individual and the race. Like religion, education provided a means of sustaining hope in an otherwise hopeless situation. In her study of Sunflower County, Hortense Powdermaker called her chapter on black schools "Education as a Faith." "Members of a race characterized by the Whites as thriftless and improvident," she wrote, "scheme and save and labor, sometimes for years in advance, to secure an education for their children. Almost every mother is ardent in her wish that her child should receive more education than she did, and thus gain the prospect of an easier and happier life." [19]

Yet was the faith of black southerners in education—and in their teachers—a cruel illusion? One only has to listen to the clichéd, anodyne speeches of today's politicians to realize that treating education as a panacea is an enduring fallacy. Ploughing through the countless speeches and articles by teachers, both black and white, during the heyday of the public school movement, one is continually struck by the naiveté of the claims advanced for education. By the 1930s, when the Great Depression bore down upon black southerners with crushing weight, the educators' boundless optimism, evangelical fervor, and self-righteous confidence seemed tragically misplaced. A torrent of sociological research painted a miserable picture of inadequacy and failure in black schools, and many now concluded, with W. E. B. Du Bois, that education could not reform and uplift the masses, could not eliminate inequality, could not eradicate prejudice, and could not even guide society.[20] If some historians of the black experience have confidently asserted that education was a means of liberation, others have hotly disputed the notion that schools did very much at all to advance the black struggle for equality. To equate education with black empowerment, they argue, invites the obvious objection that education did *not* empower black southerners. Ultimately, agitation and protest, not education and self-improvement, broke down the walls of Jim Crow.

This argument has several elements. One is that the development of black education in the South was not a story of linear progress; it was slow, haphazard, and things sometimes went from bad to worse. In the early twentieth century, for example, black schools fell even further behind the standards of white schools. The fact that educational disparities widened after blacks lost the right to vote underlines the essential point: black political power waned even as black literacy increased. J. Morgan Kousser asserts that it is irrelevant to argue that black schools improved: "In the struggle for jobs, or, more broadly, for increased economic welfare, it is *relative*, not absolute, levels of education that count." Unequal education perpetuated racial inequality.[21]

In the second place, even when black schools finally began catching up with white schools, educational gains did not lead to corresponding economic and political gains. Starting in the 1940s, black and white schools in the South moved steadily toward equalization; yet, even as the gap closed, blacks remained politically powerless and were still subjected to systematic job discrimination. By 1965, black schools had achieved near parity with white schools in terms of per capita spending, teachers' salaries, and length of school terms. But young black men were still earning 30 percent less than young white men.[22]

Here the critique of black schools merges with the wider critique of public education advanced by scholars like Michael Katz, Clarence Karier, Walter Feinberg, Ira Katznelson, Margaret Weir, Samuel Bowles, and Herbert Gintis. Put simply, their work rejects the idea that public schools have been engines of democracy and equality. They argue that as public education became professionalized, bureaucratized, and "reformed," schools actually reinforced inequalities of class, race, and gender. These "revisionist" historians of education disagree about how far teachers, reformers, education officials, and philanthropic foundations actually willed such consequences. What they do agree is that, as Bowles and Gintis argue in their classic 1976 study *Schooling in Capitalist America,* "education . . . has never been a potent force for economic equality."[23]

Equating education with liberation evokes a fourth, more complicated, objection: educational gains were rarely clear-cut. Almost every educational strategy has been double-edged, entailing conflicts, costs, and compromises. It is often hard to judge, therefore, what has constituted progress. The replacement of white teachers with black ones is a case in point. In the rural areas, the preference for black teachers often represented a bending to the wishes of local whites, who hated the "Yankee schoolmarms" but tolerated southern blacks whom they could more easily control or intimidate. "They have had a school house burnt by having a white teacher to teach them," reported a Freedmen's Bureau officer from Fayetteville, Tennessee, in 1866. A black teacher, he added, "would meet the approbation of the community at large." In the cities, by contrast, the departure of southern white teachers often caused white taxpayers and administrators to lose interest in black schools, leading to a decline in black teachers' salaries and a general waning of support. In New Orleans and Charleston, members of the largely mulatto groups that descended from the Free Negroes of antebellum times often chose to send their children to private denominational schools that retained white teachers. Catholic schools, and American Missionary Association schools, tended to attract the lighter-complexioned and the better-off.[24]

No matter how unselfishly those who acquired education committed themselves to uplifting the masses, education—and the lack of it—became sources of class identity and class tension. Some blacks wanted white teachers, explained a Freedmen's Bureau official, because "they want to learn to pronounce and speak like white persons." Yet a habit not unknown today, that of identifying education itself with "white" values, was also evident a hundred years ago. Those who learned to "speak correctly," recalled Richard Wright Jr., were "sometimes ridiculed and called 'proper' or 'white folksy.'" When educated teachers went back into the countryside, they could sometimes barely communicate with their pupils and neighbors. "The people don't know enough words for a fellow to carry on a conversation with them," complained North Carolina teacher and future novelist Charles W. Chesnutt. "He must reduce his phraseology several degrees lower than that of the first reader." But Richard Wright Jr. believed that educated blacks often lost influence with the masses by denigrating the vernacular dialect.[25]

Sometimes black teachers replaced whites only to find themselves embroiled in conflicts with ministers. During Reconstruction, black ministers often led the opposition to white teachers. Having established their independence from white-controlled denominations, ministers resented whites who criticized black worship as ignorant, superstitious, and overemotional. In Staunton, Virginia, Rev. F. W. Morris ejected a white teacher from his church and took over the classes himself. "You don't need any Northern teachers," he told the congregation, "let your own people teach you." But the church's success in extending its influence over schools did not always produce happy results, especially when teachers were caught in the crossfire between Baptists and Methodists or resisted pressure for Bible-based schooling. Charles P. Adams, who founded a school in northern Louisiana that eventually became Grambling University, contended for years against bitter opposition from Baptist ministers, who sponsored a rival school. Sectarianism encouraged duplication and unnecessary competition. Booker T. Washington—who famously charged that "a very large number of our colored ministers are morally unfit"—complained that denominational wrangling made the job of teachers even more difficult.[26]

Washington himself personifies yet another problem with the education-as-liberation thesis. Critics argued that Washington sacrificed the principle of equality in order to secure white support, and that was far too high a price to pay for separate and unequal schools. By abjuring protest, denigrating politics, and stressing "industrial education" to the detriment of broader educational opportunity, he offered a program of racial advancement that was flawed. At best, it represented an approach to social change that was almost glacial in its gradualism; at worst, it actually damaged the position of black southerners. As a program for achieving economic independence for blacks, "industrial education" was a failure. Moreover, Washington did little to disabuse his corporate and southern white backers of the notion that "industrial education" entailed the acceptance by blacks of second-class citizenship.

By the time of his death in 1915, it was painfully clear that Washington's appeasement of southern whites had done little to soften racial discrimination. True, Washington loosened the purse strings of northern philanthropists. But as many historians have pointed out, the foundations acquiesced in racial segregation and in many instances sought to strengthen white supremacy. In Louis Harlan's damning verdict on Washington, "By the white men's indirect rule, he was 'the king of a captive people.'"[27]

The position of black teachers as community leaders was therefore deeply ambiguous—some would say fatally compromised. In addition to respect, teachers also evoked cynicism and distrust. A novel by J. Saunders Redding, *Stranger and Alone,* published in 1951, offers a bitter perspective. Redding, a professor of English at Hampton Institute, gave a chilling portrait of a black teacher who possessed no idealism, no racial loyalty, and no spiritual strength; in return for preferment and privilege, he betrayed NAACP members to the white school superintendent. Indeed, betrayal and bad faith have been constant refrains in discussions of black teachers.[28]

How do we make sense of the Janus-faced literature on black education? One way is to understand that black teachers had set themselves, and had been set by others, goals that were impossible of fulfillment. Teachers were also expected to be public health workers, Sunday school teachers, home visitors, agricultural experts, fundraisers, adult literacy teachers, racial diplomats, moral examples, all-around pillars of the community, and general uplifters of the race. As Michael Fultz has written, "No other group of African American professionals . . . shouldered so many additional responsibilities considered essential to 'success' in their work, or received so much public criticism by members of their own race for their alleged failings."[29]

We must also recognize that during the Jim Crow era nearly all black southerners faced the problem of needing to appease whites while still maintaining personal dignity and racial loyalty. Teachers experienced that pressure in a particularly acute way. Unlike ministers, they depended upon white support: school improvements had to be achieved through supplication and persuasion rather than negotiation and pressure. Black teachers therefore went to great lengths to obtain white protection and approval.

In the towns and cities, white superintendents kept black principals under careful scrutiny, and looked to them as a source of information about what was going on inside the black community. Superintendents and school board members also used them as chauffeurs, gardeners, and repair men, and sometimes treated their wives as washerwomen. Arthur Harold Parker, founder and principal of Birmingham Industrial High School, studiously avoided anything that remotely smacked of politics lest he alienate whites. "He could have said one little word that might have meant a lot for the Negro in this community," complained a member of Birmingham's NAACP, "[but] he did not act . . . because his vision was so narrow. . . . He did not know that from his actions on numerous occasions he was selling the Negro out." [30]

Teachers in private schools had a little more breathing-space, but they too depended upon the goodwill of white bankers, planters, merchants, and politicians. Laurence C. Jones, who founded the famous "Piney Woods School" in Mississippi in 1909 and headed it for sixty years, eschewed anything that hinted at criticism of whites or dissatisfaction with segregation. Whenever he visited state officials in Jackson, he would don work overalls. Later, when the Civil Rights movement challenged Jim Crow, Jones could always be relied upon to assure whites that "I like things the way they are." [31]

The role of teachers as racial diplomats, therefore, made it hard for blacks to regard them with unalloyed respect. On the one hand, teachers were admired for their selfless dedication; on the other hand, their lack of militancy, and the privileged status that whites bestowed upon them, rankled. Historian John Haley's verdict on North Carolina teacher Charles N. Hunter could be extended to all such followers of Booker T. Washington: "Their advocacy of disfranchisement, their incessant denials of any desires for social equality, and their frequent pronouncements on the undesirable features of the black community . . . would have been better left unsaid. They did nothing to improve the image of their race and only served to reinforce the prejudices of whites." [32]

Yet historian Glenda Gilmore has likened the position of the black teacher to that of a "double agent." In other words, if the teacher appeared to appease whites and play the role of "Uncle Tom," it was for the larger purpose of serving the black community. The problem with "double agents," of course, is that their position requires them to play two sides against each other, and it often becomes impossible to decide where their ultimate loyalty lies. That is why, in the world of spying, the acid test of loyalty is called the "profit-and-loss account," a process in which the known good an agent has done is weighed against the suspected harm he has done. [33]

If we apply the profit-and-loss principle to the leading accommodationist, Booker T. Washington, we find that most of the damage that he allegedly wrought, notably the general deterioration in the status of black southerners, occurred independently of anything he did or said, through factors completely beyond his control. Washington's achievements, on the other hand, while falling far short of his vision, were palpably his own work: creating Tuskegee Institute, helping to found smaller schools across the South, encouraging northern capitalists to support black education, facilitating the launch of the Rosenwald school-building program, and creating a political machine that exerted influence in the highest ranks of government. More intangible, but no less important, was the pride and confidence that Washington's self-help philosophy encouraged.

The Tuskegee ethic of hard work, self-improvement, and Christian virtue may strike us as apolitical and excessively individualistic. Yet those very virtues, Washington insisted, would "give the lie to the assertion of his enemies North and South that the Negro is the inferior of the white man." For all his economic and political conservatism, Washington stoutly defended black humanity and never renounced the ultimate goal of equality. The average Negro child, he insisted, was the intellectual equal of the average white child. Blacks might be ignorant, he argued, but they were not degraded. Far from being indolent, he told whites, "the masses of the colored people work hard, but . . . someone else receives the profits." And to those who alleged that blacks had little reverence for family life, Washington replied that blacks took care of their dependents to a greater degree, perhaps, than any other race. "In all my experience in the South, I do not think I have ever seen a little child suffering by reason of the fact that no one would take him into his family." [34]

Such assertions help to explain why many white southerners never allayed their suspicion of Washington. Their hysterical reaction to his dinner with President Theodore Roosevelt in 1901 contained a basic insight: as an Arkansas schools superintendent put it, the episode betrayed Washington's "deep down antipathy to white supremacy." Another southerner, a South Carolina man, pointed out that "whenever Professor Washington aspires for the negro a place not inferior in some respects to the humblest white man's place, he challenges the embattled, inflexible and . . . unmerciful Anglo-Saxon." [35]

If Washington inwardly winced at the praise of his white racist supporters, he had little difficulty in distinguishing the lesser of the two evils. On the one hand were men like Birmingham schools superintendent John Herbert Phillips, who believed that the Negro brain stopped developing at puberty and that it was pointless to educate black youths beyond the age of 14, but who nevertheless supported an "industrial high school" for blacks; on the other hand were race-baiting politicians like James K. Vardaman, governor of Mississippi, who pronounced Negro education an abject failure and proposed to cut off state support for it. "Literary education—the knowledge of books," claimed Vardaman, "does not seem to produce any good substantial results with the Negro, but serves to sharpen his cunning, breeds hopes that cannot be fulfilled, inspires aspirations that cannot be gratified . . . promotes indolence, and in turn leads to crime." [36]

Small wonder that Washington so tirelessly advocated "industrial education," assuring whites again and again that blacks would continue to work with their hands. His belief in the importance of manual labor was genuine. But he also shrewdly calculated that de-emphasizing the literary content of black education mitigated white opposition to black schools. As he told the National Education Association in 1884, "Keep in mind the two hundred years' schooling in prejudice against the Negro which the ex-slaveholders are called upon to conquer." In practice, over half the instructors at Tuskegee Institute taught literary subjects, and the school quietly developed what one historian described as a "complicated but effective academic program . . . which provided an almost infinite number of class levels to match up with individual abilities and preparation."[37]

Harlan and other critics of Washington miss a crucial point when they emphasize the widening gap between black schools and white schools in the decades after 1900: things might have been even worse. Through skillful racial diplomacy, Washington and like-minded educators not only strengthened black private schools but also helped to fend off the threat that disfranchisement might lead to the complete extinction of black public schools. Even the attenuated schooling that survived the onslaught of triumphant white supremacy heightened blacks' consciousness of their minority status and implicitly challenged Jim Crow.

In one of the few passages of his autobiography in which he allowed his personal feelings to show, Washington struck a note of almost defiant moral superiority in discussing his racial identity:

> From any point of view, I had rather be what I am, a member of the Negro race, than be able to claim membership with the most favored of any other race. I have always been sad when I have heard members of any race claiming rights and privileges, or certain badges of distinction, on the ground simply that they were members of this or that race, regardless of their own individual worth or attainment. . . . Every persecuted individual and race should get much consolation out of the great human law, which is universal and eternal, that merit, no matter under what skin it is found, is, in the long run, recognized and rewarded. This I have said here, not to

call attention to myself as an individual, but to the race to which I am proud to belong.

As the eminent black sociologist Charles S. Johnson argued more than half a century ago, the white South *failed* to construct a true "caste system" because black people never internalized racist values. Washington and other teachers kept hope alive; however much it appeared otherwise, they were educating for equality.[38]

2 Robert R. Moton and the Travail of the Black College President

In 1916, when the trustees of Tuskegee Institute selected Robert Russa Moton to succeed Booker T. Washington, they had every reason to believe that they were choosing a black man who was, in the parlance of the day, "safe, sane, and conservative." Moton, after all, had been Washington's friend and ally. Equally important, he was an alumnus of Washington's alma mater, Hampton Institute. Founded by General Samuel Chapman Armstrong, a passionate exponent of "industrial education" for black people as well as a severe critic of black political ambitions, Hampton's ethos was even more conservative than Tuskegee's. His long tenure at Hampton as a teacher suggested that "Major" Moton—a military title acquired by commanding the school's cadet corps—could be relied upon to accept the guidance of white paternalists.[1]

In his inaugural address as president of Tuskegee, Moton faithfully affirmed the wisdom of the school's founder. Black people would advance, said Moton, through education, honest toil, and harmonious cooperation with whites—"Not by arrogant self-seeking, not by bluff, sham, or bombast, not by fault-finding, not by shirking at difficulty, or shirking from duty, [and] not by the cherishing of prejudice against the white man." For good measure, Moton threw in a Washingtonian complaint that "ignorance, shiftlessness, disease, insufficiency and crime are entirely too prevalent among our people."[2]

A few days later, Moton's commitment to conciliating the white South at all costs was put to an excruciatingly painful test. His wife, Jennie, was ejected from a Pullman railway car while traveling through Alabama. White passengers objected to her presence aboard the luxury sleeping-car, and, when she refused to move, a policeman boarded the train at Troy and escorted her to the segregated colored carriage. The incident was national news. Yet Moton did not protest his wife's treatment and condemn segregation in interstate travel—for black people, perhaps the most detested manifestation of Jim Crow. Rather, he swallowed this insult to his wife and remained silent. "It were better I had never been born," he confided to one southern white man, "than to change the pleasant equilibrium between the races which Mr. Washington so wisely and successfully established."[3]

Many whites applauded Moton's stoicism. One letter of support came from a man who described himself as a "dyed-in-the-wool Southerner . . . possessing all the prejudice-breeding attitudes." More revealing, perhaps, was praise from Seth Low, a former mayor of New York and president of Columbia University. Low conceded that while segregation might inconvenience "the few refined and educated Negroes . . . the separation of the races on the trains is not in itself a thing to be condemned without reserve." Indeed, Low was convinced that "race purity is as strong an instinct at the North as it is at the South."[4]

The fact that Seth Low personified the civic virtue of northern reformers, and that he served diligently on Tuskegee's board of trustees, prompts an unkind reflection: With friends like this, did blacks in the South need enemies? Yet the support of socially respected, politically connected mugwumps such as Low was vital for Tuskegee's survival and growth. The school's ability to attract money from robber barons and philanthropists—the two were often the same—depended upon it. And the plain fact was that the northern benefactors of black education for the most part accepted the white South's insistence that racial segregation—accompanied by disfranchisement—was the only workable solution to Dixie's race problem.

This brings us to the crux of the matter. Education for second-class citizenship was, in the eyes of some blacks at the time—and in the opinion of many historians since—no education at all. If the cost of white philanthropy was acceptance of white supremacy, then

Rockefeller, Carnegie, and Rosenwald money came in a poisoned chalice. Among blacks in the North especially, Moton was scorned as an appeaser in the same way that Washington had been condemned for selling out the race.

The question went far beyond education. Washington and Moton both fulfilled broader functions as race leaders, and their roles were in large part defined by whites. If Moton was a man of lesser influence than Washington, he nonetheless enjoyed similar access to white men of wealth and power. Like Washington, he was consulted by the foundations; like Washington, he became an advisor to presidents. As John Barry puts it in *Rising Tide,* his account of the 1927 Mississippi flood, "Moton was the white man's biggest Negro." [5]

Inheriting Washington's role, however, also meant inheriting the quarrel between Washington and W. E. B. Du Bois, a bitter dispute that had polarized black leadership into opposing camps. More conciliatory than Washington, Moton wanted to end the cold war between the "Tuskegee machine" and the NAACP. But if the personal animus sustaining the quarrel died with Washington, the underlying issues—northern leadership versus southern leadership, protest versus accommodationism—refused to go away.

The publication in 1916 of *Negro Education,* a two-volume survey of black schools and colleges, provided Du Bois with more ammunition in his battle against the "Tuskegee Idea." Written by Thomas Jesse Jones, a Welsh immigrant who studied at Columbia University, taught at Hampton Institute, and became director of the Phelps-Stokes Fund, *Negro Education* was scathing about academic standards at black universities. On the other hand, Jones praised Tuskegee Institute and pleaded for more "industrial education." To Du Bois, Jones personified the bossy paternalism and political conservatism of the northern philanthropic foundations. It also made him suspicious of Robert Moton, whom Jones and the Phelps-Stokes Fund built up as the model Negro leader. It was not long before Du Bois saw fit to attack Moton himself. [6]

The occasion for Du Bois's attack was Moton's trip to France in

1919, undertaken at the behest of the War Department to investigate unrest among, and complaints against, black troops. It is important, however, to outline its context. America's entry into the First World War had encouraged hopes of great change among blacks; it also nurtured a new crop of radicals. Challenged from the left by younger men like A. Philip Randolph, Du Bois needed a conservative foil more than ever. His own prestige, moreover, had suffered when it became known that his super-patriotic *Crisis* editorial, "Close Ranks," which called upon blacks to set aside their grievances for the duration of the war, might have been linked with his own desire for an Army commission. Having failed to secure the hoped-for commission, Du Bois needed to redeem his radical credentials.[7]

In typically combative style, Du Bois used the pages of *Crisis*, the NAACP's magazine, to blast Moton. He claimed that Moton was less interested in uncovering discrimination than in telling the Negro troops how to comport themselves when they returned to America. Moton allegedly advised the soldiers to forget about gaining the right to vote or upsetting Jim Crow. As if to clinch his case, Du Bois added that "[Moton] took with him and had at his elbow every moment that evil genius of the Negro race, Thomas Jesse Jones, a white man."[8]

As usual, Du Bois exaggerated. Nevertheless, his attack hit home. Millions of blacks seethed with indignation over Moton's speech to the colored soldiers. One wrote to Moton to express his disgust: "You ought to have gone over and fired the boys with the thought that they . . . demand their rights as men and citizens. The rights of a white man. Equal rights. . . . They say you are 'white folks nigger.' That you are in the gang that helps to keep the Negro down." When, after the war, Moton joined with southern white liberals to form the Commission on Interracial Cooperation, Du Bois dismissed the effort as yet another strategy to keep blacks in their place, and he labeled Moton a "pussy footer."[9]

Working with white people who believed in segregation—and there were few whites who did not—could be justified as a means to an end. Conforming to Jim Crow could be defended as a practical necessity. But the Great War, the Garvey movement, and then the Great Depression encouraged blacks to think that white supremacy was vulnerable; the accommodationism of Moton and others like him appeared to be shoring up a system that was not only indefensible but also rotting.

In the 1920s student rebellions rocked black campuses, challenging the authority of traditionally autocratic college presidents. In the 1930s black intellectuals attacked southern college presidents as practitioners of a bankrupt strategy—one that failed the black community but rewarded "Uncle Toms." Lewis K. McMillan, who taught history at South Carolina State College, complained that "The [black college] president is usually an ignorant autocrat" who "stands a surer chance of keeping his job to the extent that he is hostile to the best interests of his own people." When such men acted as community leaders, observed J. Saunders Redding of Hampton Institute, "there rises a nauseating reek of devious and oily obsequiousness. It is a kind of fascism in reverse." [10]

Oily obsequiousness was most visible, perhaps, at the annual open days, when white visitors to black colleges were stuffed with mouthwatering food, treated to elaborate entertainments, and pampered with fawning attention. Black students often bitterly resented these displays. On one occasion in the 1930s, for example, students at Kentucky State College were told to wear bandannas and to mime the actions of slaves picking cotton while they sang spirituals for their distinguished visitors. The students adamantly refused to don the brightly colored head-rags. The very act of singing spirituals was regarded, by some, as demeaning. Ever since the Fisk Jubilee Singers took the North and Europe by storm in the 1870s, black colleges had been sending choirs on fundraising tours. But white audiences often expected the songs to be performed in a certain way; as a member of the Tuskegee Institute quartet complained, whites wanted them to shout and moan, to "'play the Nigger'—their own words—more." In 1926 Hampton students initiated a protest strike by refusing to sing spirituals in front of a visiting British colonial official. [11]

In one of the great set-pieces of modern American literature, embedded in the novel *Invisible Man*, Ralph Ellison wrote a hilarious satire of an open day at a fictional college that was, unmistakably, Tuskegee Institute. The climax of Ellison's tour-de-force comes when the college's president, Dr. Bledsoe, berates the novel's anonymous protagonist, a naive student, for inadvertently exposing Mr. Norton, a white trustee from Boston, to the seamier side of black life. This beyond-the-tracks diversion included a visit to a shack inhabited by an incestuous family and a trip to a brothel patronized by shell-shocked mental patients from the Negro Veterans Hospital.

Unburdening himself in the privacy of his office, Dr. Bledsoe explained to the student his philosophy of leadership:

> I'se big and black and I say "Yes, suh" as loudly as any burrhead when it's convenient, but I'm still the king down here. I don't care how much it appears otherwise. Power doesn't have to show off. Power is confident, self-assuring, self-starting and self-stopping, self-warming and self-justifying. When you have it, you know it. Let the Negroes snicker and the crackers laugh! Those are the facts, son. The only ones I even pretend to please are *big* white folk, and even those I control more than they control me. This is a power set-up, son, and I'm at the controls.

Ellison's point, of course, is that such power was also self-serving: as Bledsoe cynically admits, "I'll have every Negro in the country hanging on tree limbs in the morning if it means staying where I am." [12] If this were the true story, and the whole story, then one could readily agree with poet Langston Hughes that southern black colleges were "doing their best to produce spineless Uncle Toms," and conclude that men like Robert Moton were race traitors. [13]

It is a mistake, however, to confuse fiction with fact. As Horace Mann Bond wrote Ellison in 1967, "I thought of Dr. Bledsoe as a sort of composite, not as an intended portrait of the typical Negro college president; and I thought you laid it on a little thick." Bond, who spent six years as president of Fort Valley State College in Georgia, added that Ellison's reference to Bledsoe's *two* Cadillacs was scarcely credible: he never knew a college president to own even one. Black college presidents drove Buicks, Chryslers, Studebakers, and Packards: "The boys . . . had too much sense to be caught driving a Cadillac around in the rural South." [14]

Actually, Bond was wrong about the car—Moton did own a big Cadillac, courtesy of the National Negro Business League. But his essential point was correct. Robert Russa Moton was not Dr. Bledsoe. Moton sought power not for self-aggrandizement but for the benefit of Tuskegee Institute, for the improvement of black education, and for progress toward racial equality. The last goal was sometimes disguised, often compromised, and more evident in his private than his public actions. But it was consistent, and Moton pursued it doggedly and sometimes courageously. Yes, Moton accommodated to southern segregation. But he never accepted the racist rationale for Jim Crow, and he never envisaged segregation as a natural or permanent condition. [15]

A tall, sturdy man of dark complexion, Moton possessed a quiet dignity that bespoke inner strength. His belief in racial equality stemmed from education and experience, and rested as well upon pride in his roots. Family tradition held that the first of his ancestors to be enslaved by white men was an African chief who, in the process of selling some captives of a rival tribe, was himself kidnapped by the slavers. Of his own father, Moton recalled a powerfully built man who once overpowered his slave overseer when the latter attempted to whip him. According to Moton, his father extracted a promise from his master that he should not be whipped again. "My father used to say that one man could not chastise another. . . . That idea was very strong in his mind." Of his mother, Moton recalled "a woman of very strong character" who turned her cabin into a freedmen's school after the Civil War. [16]

Read one way, many of Moton's statements seemed to pander to his white audiences. For example, when he asserted that blacks came through slavery "with much to [their] credit," while whites had reaped "disadvantages from which the whole country still suffers," he appeared to echo the anti-abolitionist sentiments of southern historians like U. B. Phillips. But an alternative reading reveals something different: a tone of superiority—a belief that bondage had, morally at least, corrupted the masters and fortified the slaves. Like his predecessor, Booker T. Washington, Robert Moton often charmed southern white audiences in a manner that outraged men like Du Bois. Yet Moton also had a subtle gift for making a point about equality—and even gently needling his listeners. As his successor, Fred Patterson, noted, "His tact and grace made it possible to deliver what could have been interpreted by white Southerners as a stiff rebuke in a manner that made his pronouncements not only acceptable, but also effective." [17]

Moton's speech before the 1929 convention of the National Education Association exemplified the technique. "I am somewhat embarrassed this morning," he began, "but I don't want to embarrass you. This platform and auditorium are not lacking in character and dignity. I think they are somewhat lacking in color. I shall not attempt to add anything in the way of dignity or character . . . but I am perfectly sure I will bring more color than any other speaker." (Moton, one should remember, was a very dark-complexioned man.) One cringes, today, to read such "jokes," but the more perceptive teachers in the audience would have accompanied their chuckles with an uncomfortable reflection: Moton was criticizing the NEA for being a Jim Crow organization. Later on in the speech, Moton referred to the Great War in terms that doubtless made his audience squirm: "We don't think we are an inferior race. . . . The fact is that about ten years ago I thought the whole nordic race, the whole group of white races were backward the way they were killing each other, murdering each other, tearing down the achievements of art, and literature, and science." [18]

Most of the time, Moton pursued his cause in private, seeking to influence whites with calm reason, knowing that angry rhetoric would merely alienate them. He suffered fools gladly. When a Methodist missionary from the North, bound for central Africa, inquired about the "characteristics of the negro race as a race," Moton replied carefully. "As you probably know"—this man plainly did not—"the leading anthropological authorities are saying that there is no such thing as race per se, and to illustrate this . . . they are pointing to the great diversity of peoples found in North Africa." When a factory owner from Michigan sought "two reliable and cooperative colored servants," Moton tactfully explained that Tuskegee was not a school for training cooks and maids, nor was it an employment agency.[19]

More important, Moton used his reputation as a black conservative to nudge white leaders away from their complacent belief that the race problem could be solved on the basis of segregation and disfranchisement. Meeting with Woodrow Wilson in June 1918, Moton urged the president to speak out against lynching and mob violence and to call upon state governors to suppress it. There was more restlessness among colored people than ever before, he warned Wilson; with every instance of racial violence, disaffection and radicalism mounted.[20]

As the NAACP made lynching the centerpiece of its campaigning, Moton cooperated with the organization that his predecessor had despised and conspired against. The NAACP was agitating for a federal law against lynching, and the issue, which to many southern whites raised the specter of Yankee bayonets trampling on states' rights, was political dynamite. Moton supported the campaign but bit his tongue. In 1922, however, with the public debate at fever pitch, he vented his feelings to James Hardy Dillard, a former classics professor from Tulane University who now headed the Jeanes Fund, a philanthropic foundation dedicated to improving black schools. The gentlemanly Dillard told Moton that he opposed the anti-lynching bill on the grounds that it would be unenforceable, and would merely antagonize white southerners. "I am mighty glad to get your judgment on the . . . lynching situation," Moton replied.[21]

Moton then proceeded to tell the good doctor that he emphatically disagreed. Imagine the pall of fear that lynching produced, he asked Dillard. "I, or any one of us, may be taken from a train or elsewhere and lynched without Judge or jury, should we come near the description as given of a Negro charged with a crime in that locality. . . . Our most intelligent and upright Negroes are ever conscious of the fact that at any hour they may be hurled into eternity." Lynching created more bitterness among blacks, and more hatred against white people, than anything else—including disfranchisement, segregation, and unequal education, bad as those things were. "I am so strong in my feeling against lynching that . . . I feel there should be some power, somewhere, that could and would see to it that a man charged with crime, whatever the crime, should be guaranteed a trial." If the states, after fifty years of lynching, would not do this, then the federal government should. As for states' rights, Moton pointed out that the South had thrown that doctrine to the winds by supporting Prohibition.[22]

When he wrote that letter in 1922, most of the "whites of good will" who sought to alleviate the Negro's condition thought that disfranchisement and segregation were necessary and sensible. The difficulty facing men like Moton was to work with these liberals in the cause of racial peace while at the same time trying to persuade them that peace without equality was a chimera. This frustrating task required tremendous patience.

One of Moton's most important backers, for example, was the Phelps-Stokes Fund, a powerful ally in the battle for philanthropic money. The men who headed the Fund, however, believed that blacks should adjust to Jim Crow, not challenge it. The Fund's president, Anson Phelps Stokes, felt so strongly about this that he challenged a biography of Booker T. Washington, written by his former secretary Emmett J. Scott, for failing to note that Washington had regretted dining with President Theodore Roosevelt at the White House in 1901—an incident that outraged southern whites. Scott adamantly denied that Washington had ever regarded his dinner with Roosevelt as a mistake. The point seems trivial, but it had huge symbolic importance. Stokes wished blacks to accept his view that segregation was wise and permanent; Scott and Moton insisted that it was unjust and should end. In like fashion, the white members of the Commission on Interracial Cooperation wanted to ignore the issue of black disfranchisement. Moton argued that the CIC had to take it up.[23]

Of all the incidents in Moton's life, there is no better illustration of the conditions that circumscribed his leadership than the dedication of the Lincoln Memorial in Washington D.C. on May 30, 1922. The only black speaker on a platform that included President Warren G. Harding, Moton wanted to include a stinging denunciation of racial discrimination. The original draft of his speech included the following words:

> I say unto you that this memorial which we erect is but a hollow mockery, a symbol of hypocrisy, unless we can make real in our national life, in every state and in every section, the things for which [Lincoln] died. . . . Sometimes I think the national government itself has not always set the best example for the states in this regard.
>
> A government which can venture abroad to put an end to injustice and mob violence in another country can surely find a way to put an end to these same evils within our own borders. . . . Twelve million black men and women . . . are proud of their American citizenship, but they are determined that it shall mean for them no less than any other group, the largest enjoyment of opportunity and the fullest blessings of freedom.

The speech that Moton actually delivered, however, had been drastically censored by the Lincoln Memorial Commission, chaired by Chief Justice and former president William Howard Taft. The reproach to the national government went out; the charge of national hypocrisy disappeared; the reference to a nation "half yet in bondage" vanished. Instead, Moton marveled at the progress of racial cooperation and understanding—especially in the South—and stressed that blacks were loyal and useful citizens. Still, of all the speakers that day, Moton was the only one to allude, albeit tentatively, to racial discrimination. He managed to salvage something.[24]

That Moton acquiesced in the censoring of his speech is not that surprising. Confrontation was not his style. Moreover, William Howard Taft was a longtime trustee of Hampton Institute whom Moton knew well. Equally to the point, Moton's loyalty to the Republican party and his perceived influence with black voters gave him access to the White House and influence with the federal government. To spoil a Republican celebration at the Lincoln dedication would have been senseless. By staying in the party's good graces, on the other hand, he might yet achieve some advantage for his race.

Moton's loyalty paid off when President Harding agreed to build a Veterans Bureau hospital for black ex-soldiers and to locate it in Tuskegee. Moreover, over the bitter opposition of many Alabama whites and despite brazen obstructionism from officials in the Veterans Bureau, Harding fulfilled a promise to Moton that the hospital would be staffed and administered entirely by blacks. The Tuskegee Institute faced down threats of violence, including a parade by the Ku Klux Klan, while armed guards protected the campus. "I sat with [Moton] in his home at Tuskegee during the height of the trouble," recalled the NAACP's Walter White. "He pointed to a rifle and a shotgun, well oiled and grimly businesslike, that stood in a corner. . . . 'I've got only one time to die. If I must die now to save Tuskegee Institute, I'm ready. I've been running long enough.'" Blacks across America applauded Moton's stand.[25]

Pete Daniel entitled his account of the affair "Black Power in the 1920s." Here was a case of blacks campaigning for and securing a segregated institution that provided training, employment, and services for black people. Moreover, as Desmond King notes, blacks chalked up this gain—worth $75,000 a month in terms of payroll alone—at a time when they were at the nadir of their political strength and winning precious few victories anywhere. Why the anomaly? The answer, perhaps, is that if any black leader could wrest concessions from a Republican president, it was Robert R. Moton.[26]

Whether that constituted "power" or merely "influence" is a fine point. An incident from 1931, however, is illuminating. When President Herbert Hoover promised to speak at Tuskegee's fiftieth anniversary but then canceled, Moton was understandably annoyed. He had helped Hoover, when the latter was Secretary of Commerce, deal with the Great Mississippi Flood of 1927; he had rallied black support for Hoover in the 1928 campaign; he had chaired a government commission on Haiti, appointed by Hoover after he became president. Moton now reminded Hoover that his visit to Tuskegee "would have a vitally strategic influence in the next presidential campaign." He then warned Hoover in no uncertain terms that "many leaders among us . . . question not only the good faith of the party of which you are leader, but also your personal concern for the welfare and progress of one-tenth of the citizenship of our country." Hoover decided to visit Tuskegee after all.[27]

Party loyalty, therefore, had to serve a purpose, and Moton did not shrink from calling in his political IOUs. In 1931 he demanded that Hoover stop the War Department from dispersing the Army's four black regiments "solely to do menial work for white soldiers." Treating blacks as laborers rather than combat troops would be "a grave injustice and unwarranted humiliation against the Negro race." Two years later, Moton tried to persuade Hoover to promote black smallholdings by providing sharecroppers with low-interest government loans. However, this ambitious plan to break up the South's big plantations—and to combat the influence of the Communist-backed Sharecroppers Union—came to nothing.[28]

Moton had no illusions about the Republican party's concern for the Negro. At his first meeting with Warren Harding, he was astonished by that politician's ignorance of racial matters and appalled by his profane language. ("If you eliminated the word 'damn' from that man's vocabulary," one person noted, "he could do nothing but stutter.") Coolidge and Hoover disappointed him mightily. In fact, Moton considered most Republicans "genuine political hypocrites" when it came to race. Hoover's defeat in 1932 was no bad thing, because "The sooner the country . . . realizes the Negro doesn't have on a Republican or a Democratic collar and that he is doing his own thinking, the better it will be for the Negro and . . . for the nation."[29]

Moton had come a long way from the accommodationism of Booker T. Washington. In 1925 the Tuskegee Institute began college work, thus ending the longstanding dispute between advocates of "industrial" education and supporters of "higher" education. Four years later Moton published *What the Negro Thinks*, in which he insisted that black people opposed enforced segregation, condemned injustice in the courts, and keenly resented discrimination in jobs, housing, and education—in short, they desired full equality. Moton's views were now so close to those of the NAACP that the Association awarded him its highest honor, the Spingarn Medal.[30]

Moton was, of course, moving with the times—even Booker T. Washington might have achieved a rapprochement with the NAACP had he lived another ten or fifteen years. And the move away from "industrial" education was inevitable: with state education officials insisting upon higher academic standards for black teachers, Tuskegee had to offer college-level courses in order to survive. Still, Moton displayed great skill in achieving an honorable compromise between the exigencies of white supremacy and the black aspiration to equality. "In his own way he did everything possible to advance his race," writes John Barry, "and in a most difficult time he danced a most delicate dance."[31]

And so did the majority of black college presidents. Again, one must recall the constraints under which they labored. Washington had freed Tuskegee Institute from state control by building up a substantial private endowment. But state colleges had no such autonomy, and the men who headed them were at the mercy of white politicians. E. L. Blackshear of Prairie View College, Texas, was dismissed for being on the wrong side of the temperance question. Thomas DeSaille Tucker, president of Florida Colored Normal School, was fired for appointing too many northern teachers who, allegedly, sneered at "southern institutions" and instilled in their students contempt for "the agricultural and industrial life of the race." Richard R. Wright, longtime president of Georgia State Industrial College in Savannah, was told to stop teaching Latin. He eventually found race relations so oppressive that he quit the South altogether—founding a bank in Philadelphia and living to affluent old age.[32]

The harsh climate of white supremacy therefore honed the survival skills of black teachers, encouraging a mixture of circumspection and guile. When John J. Coss, a board member of the Rosenwald Fund and professor of philosophy at Columbia University, visited Georgia in 1936, he was struck by the "roundabout fashion in which by various subterfuges Negro education has been improved." He cited the example of William M. Hubbard, principal of a two-year normal school in Forsyth. Described by Coss as "slow, soft-spoken, plodding but patient and humble and beloved by many of the white townsfolk," Hubbard was particularly adept at cultivating the principal of a white Baptist girls college. He sent his boys to do odd jobs at the college and, in return, received periodic donations of dog-eared books and worn-out equipment. Behind their ingratiating façade, however, men like Hubbard were often astute diplomats. They used their connections with northern supporters—church boards, philanthropic foundations, and wealthy individuals—to manipulate state officials and leverage increased funding.[33]

Of all the South's black college presidents, the Rev. Joseph W. Holley may well have been the most conservative. Holley persuaded local whites to support the Albany (Georgia) Bible and Manual Training Institute by promising to turn out well-trained domestic servants and efficient farm laborers. He regarded white goodwill as paramount, and had no qualms about allying with race-baiting politicians like Gene Talmadge. While he was a student in the 1940s, black newspaperman A. C. Searles used to act as Holley's chauffeur. "One day, after a year or so of this, while I was driving him somewhere, I said, 'Since there ain't nobody here but us, tell me the truth.

You don't believe deep down in your heart all those things you say to white folks to raise money, do you?' He said, 'I certainly do.' He said, 'The good white folks are the best friends the Negroes ever had.' Can you believe that? Sometimes I wanted to puke over some of the things that man said." [34]

The remarkable thing, in retrospect, is that so few black college presidents went as far as Holley in endorsing white supremacy. As Kenneth Warlick discovered when he studied North Carolina history, most black college presidents contradicted the "Uncle Tom" stereotype: they were moderates rather than conservatives, and they forthrightly insisted that blacks should receive the same kind of education as that provided to whites. That was true in the state-funded institutions as well. Even when whites controlled the purse strings, "Conformity and conservatism . . . proved difficult to guarantee." [35]

While proclaiming their support for "industrial education," black college heads quietly and steadily raised academic standards. In 1908, for example, Sam Huston College in Austin, Texas, a private school founded by Reuben S. Lovinggood, boasted courses in sewing, millinery, dressmaking, cooking, housekeeping, and printing. In the college catalog, Lovinggood dismissed "Political harangues, opera house speeches, and constitutional amendments" and called instead for "prayer, patience, quiet demeanor, and a spirit of good will." Five years later Lovinggood advertised a college course by stating, "We must have prophets, priests, seers, poets, philosophers, artists, physicians, [and] orators." Even the most conservative college presidents moved in the same direction. By 1927, for example, Joseph W. Holley's school in Albany had evolved into a state-supported college with a three-year liberal arts program. [36]

Black college presidents resorted to evasions and compromises, some of them humiliating. But the benefits of what they wrought outweighed the costs. Most obviously, they increased the educational opportunities available to southern black youth: the number of black college students steadily increased, from 12,000 in 1928 to

37,000 in 1941 and 74,000 in 1950. The NAACP deplored the fact that this expansion took place within the framework of segregation, arguing that Jim Crow colleges would always be inferior. Yet black college presidents had long worked on the principle that a bird in the hand is worth two in the bush. Fred Patterson recalled that "I was loudly accused of promoting segregation" when he acquired a veterinary school for Tuskegee Institute. In his own defense, however, he pointed out that in 1944 it was the only veterinary school in the South open to blacks.[37]

Black colleges also provided intellectual space for staff and students to develop a critique of white supremacy. Although college teachers undoubtedly exercised a degree of self-censorship, they exposed students to all manner of ideas—in politics, economics, education, sociology, history, and literature—that encouraged critical thinking. In practice, whites rarely paid much attention to what went on inside black college classrooms. At Morehouse College, students could even take a class on "Karl Marx and the Negro"![38]

The idea that black colleges turned out generations of conservative school teachers—little Booker T. Washingtons—is a myth. Even in the most conformist institutions, students of education could hardly avoid that great philosopher of democracy, John Dewey. The student essays of Urissa Rhone Brown, a Texas schoolteacher who attended Prairie View in the 1940s, provide a useful insight into the educational ethos of the time:

> Those of us who took a course in Negro history a few years ago have only to remember our talks on 'the little brown brother' and the 'white man's burden' to see how many were guilty of supporting racial superiority. To my way of thinking, there is no essential mental differences in races. Differences may exist but these are so tied up with conditions of life that racial comparisons are valueless.

In a term paper on school administration, Brown argued that if the basic aim of the school was to prepare children for democracy, the school itself must set an example. "The school cannot be the cradle of democracy if this cradle is rocked by school officials and employees who are autocratic."[39]

Many black colleges permitted and even encouraged political activity outside the classroom. It comes as something of a shock to encounter Marcus Garvey speaking at Tuskegee Institute, at the invitation of Robert Moton, *after* he had been indicted by the federal government for mail fraud. Bishop College in Marshall, Texas, abandoned the traditional daily chapel service in favor of a "modernized program" that included, in 1932, a talk by Socialist leader Norman Thomas. At Paine College in Augusta, Georgia, students and faculty members produced a leaflet entitled "You Are a Citizen," with the aim of encouraging blacks to vote. The impact of the Scottsboro affair was evident in a 1934 meeting of North Carolina college administrators to discuss "What Should be the Relationship of the Negro College Students to . . . the ILD [the International Labor Defense, a Communist organization] and the NAACP?" Private colleges, with their greater freedom, were more tolerant of political activity. Yet even at state colleges in the deep South students could hear the likes of Paul Robeson, Langston Hughes, and W. E. B. Du Bois.[40]

Handling outside speakers sometimes required considerable tact. Du Bois once shared a platform at Tuskegee Institute with Jessie Daniel Ames, a southern white woman who campaigned against lynching but whose organization excluded blacks. Ames outlined her message of genteel reform, and then Du Bois lulled his listeners to sleep with a long, boring speech. The audience woke up, however, when Du Bois finished with an impassioned peroration condemning segregation and discrimination.

> The audience . . . applauded him. Du Bois took his seat. Everybody was now waiting. The chapel was dead silent, waiting for Dr. Moton to close the meeting. People asked themselves, "What's he going to say about what Dr. Du Bois said? What's he going to say about what Jesse Daniel Ames

said?" Dr. Moton got up, stood at the front of the platform, and hesitated for a few moments. Then he said, "That was a great game we had yesterday!"

A great roar engulfed the chapel.[41]

Black colleges also provided social space that helped students to acquire a sense of individual and collective efficacy. While hardly models of democracy, they were oases of freedom compared to the surrounding society. Students complained about Victorian codes of conduct, but the very frequency of student protests suggests that black colleges were not nearly as autocratic as some critics charged. When students at Tuskegee Institute went on strike in 1940 demanding better food, Fred Patterson let them run the cafeteria. The students learned a valuable lesson in economics, gladly relinquishing control after a few days. But the strike also taught something to Patterson, who thereafter made a point of including students on college committees. A few years later, Ralph David Abernathy led a similar protest at Alabama State College. President H. C. Trenholm ended the protest by promising better food. "You can deal with the most awesome authority on an equal basis," Abernathy discovered, "if the people are on your side."[42]

Black colleges produced scholarly research that helped change the conventional wisdom about race and influenced whites in positions of power. The careful, patient research of Monroe Work made Tuskegee Institute the principal source of information on lynching. Charles S. Johnson turned Fisk University into the nation's leading center of expertise on race relations. Howard University Law School, established by Charles H. Houston, trained the civil rights lawyers who won the *Brown* decision. E. Franklin Frazier, also at Howard, produced studies of the black family that influenced two generations of sociologists and helped to shape government policies into the 1960s.

Finally, black colleges fostered organizations that tried to change race relations directly. Robert Moton was a leading light in the Commission on Interracial Cooperation. Fred Patterson, his successor, contradicted his conservative reputation by supporting the leftist Southern Negro Youth Congress, which held its 1942 meeting on the campus of Tuskegee Institute. Mary McLeod Bethune founded the National Council of Negro Women and supported the biracial Southern Conference on Human Welfare. Charles S. Johnson, Benjamin Mays, and Gordon Blaine Hancock were instrumental in forming the Southern Regional Council.[43]

But when the Civil Rights movement attacked segregation head-on, black college administrators found themselves in the firing line. The demand for integration threatened their institutions; student militancy jeopardized their jobs. In 1956, when the White Citizens Council of Orangeburg, South Carolina, directed economic pressure against blacks who petitioned for school integration, students at South Carolina State College countered by boycotting the town's white merchants. President Benner C. Turner expelled the leaders of the protest, prompting students to hang him in effigy. Four years later, when the student sit-in movement swept through southern campuses, other college presidents carried out similar purges.[44]

The papers of H. C. Trenholm document the excruciating pressure faced by a black college president when the Civil Rights movement arrived on campus in 1960. Many whites were so outraged by the student-inspired sit-ins that they would happily have shut down Alabama State College, fired all its teachers, and sent its students packing. "YOU could have controlled your students," a Chattanooga man rebuked Trenholm. "YOU and your faculty evidently approve of what they do and even encourage them. You deserve and will have the ill will and even the hatred of the white people." Governor John Patterson ordered Trenholm to fire Lawrence Reddick, a history professor, "before sundown." The state board of education told him immediately to suspend thirty-one students. Trenholm balked, but he eventually expelled nine students and dismissed Reddick.[45]

Letters and telegrams then poured in from outraged African Americans. From Chicago: "It is indeed unfortunate that you have become the hatchet man for the governor of Alabama and expelled those kids from Alabama State College." From Philadelphia: "The Uncle Toms are supposed to be dead and those that are leaders are supposed to be out front carrying the banner of freedom, dignity and justice for all. How do you stand? Does economic security mean so much? How will you face tomorrow?" From Huntsville, Alabama: "We must not jump every time the white man speaks. We must stand firm for our Master's reign on high." And from a cousin in Dayton, Ohio: "You should have resigned yourself." [46]

Those who knew both Trenholm and Alabama were less harsh in their judgments. They recognized Trenholm's selfless dedication to Alabama State College, his work in promoting scholarships for black students, his decades of service to the American Teachers Association, his dogged efforts to document educational inequalities, and his quiet support for the Montgomery bus boycott. Some knew, as well, that Trenholm did not give in to Patterson without putting up a fight. When state investigators asked to see Lawrence Reddick's personnel file, Trenholm refused to produce it. Patterson eventually obtained the file, but he "had to make an issue out of it." A year later, when Alabama's director of public safety wrote for information about Fred Shuttlesworth and Ralph Abernathy, civil rights leaders and former students, Trenholm filed the letter and never replied. Such acts of quiet defiance incensed Governor Patterson and ensured Trenholm's early retirement. He died in 1963, having worked and worried himself into an early grave. [47]

George R. Woolfolk, a history professor at Prairie View College, complained that men like Trenholm were dominated by an amoral "survival psychosis" that resulted in "intellectual and spiritual sterility." Yet was their desire to save black colleges so worthy of condemnation? Those institutions were part of the sinew, brains, and soul of the black community. Back in the 1880s, Alabama State College had actually been abolished by action of the state legislature. Before regaining its charter it had survived by holding classes in the Dexter Avenue Baptist Church. Over the decades the link between the college and the church endured and grew stronger; Trenholm was attending Dexter when its pastor, Martin Luther King Jr., led the Montgomery bus boycott. For Trenholm, being a college president was more than a job, more even than a lifetime's work. But in defending the institution that he and his father had built up for half a century, Trenholm incurred the obloquy of the Civil Rights movement. As he once lamented, "Being in the field of education and also being a Negro, it seems to me to be tragic."[48]

The passage of time should make us more sympathetic to the claim of men like Trenholm that their educational work was as worthy, in its own way, as the actions of the Civil Rights movement. A Mississippi educator, Jacob Reddix, wrote in his memoirs:

> I have never personally participated in an organized protest. . . . For more than fifty years I have devoted my life to the education and enlightenment of young people. . . . During my twenty-seven years as president of Jackson State College, the institution has granted upward of 5,000 degrees to its students. I believe this contribution is as important as participating in organized protests.

Special pleading? Perhaps. Self-serving? Obviously. Yet not devoid of a certain truth. Forty years after the Civil Rights movement, the historically black college of the South faces an uncertain future. Yet for well over a century it served, in the words of Horace Mann Bond, as a "true citadel of an uncommon American tradition: that of radical acceptance of the principle of human equality."[49]

3 Black Teachers and the Civil Rights Movement

The black men and women who led the racial revolution of the 1950s and 1960s often testified to the inspirational influence of teachers. A few, usually people who were already middle-aged in the 1950s, had been taught by white people, in private schools that had been founded by northern missionaries in the late nineteenth century. Rosa Parks, whose act of quiet refusal sparked the Montgomery bus boycott, never went beyond eighth grade, but she did attend Montgomery Industrial School for Girls, an elementary school started in 1886 by two New England women. Housed in an antebellum mansion, the school enrolled over three hundred girls and employed ten teachers, all of them white women. "What I learned best," Rosa Parks remembered, "was that I was a person with dignity and self-respect, and I should not set my sights lower than anybody else just because I was black."[1]

By the 1930s white teachers who taught black children were few and far between. As the South's public school system expanded, the white-run missionary schools either closed their doors or were taken over by local school boards. And in the public schools, segregation was the inflexible rule. Yet black teachers also created centers of excellence, likewise inspiring their charges to lift their eyes beyond the horizon. Fred L. Shuttlesworth, a diminutive black minister of legendary courage who led the Civil Rights movement in Birmingham, attended a small elementary school in Oxmoor, Alabama. He derived the same kind of confidence from his black teachers that Rosa Parks had gained from her white ones. "I believed in them and they believed in me," he remembered. "These were the people from whom I learned to analyze things."[2]

Andrew Young, whose stellar career included service in the Civil Rights movement as an aide to Martin Luther King Jr., attended Valena C. Jones Junior High and Normal School in the late 1930s. The red paint that coated its exterior, and the school's location in a particularly rough neighborhood of New Orleans, earned it the nickname "Bucket of Blood." Nevertheless, Valena C. Jones bore the strong imprint of one of the outstanding black teachers of the day. Fannie C. Williams, Young recalled, was

> A handsome, dark-skinned woman with pressed, white hair, [who] believed in strict discipline and patrolled the halls of the three-story structure observing classes and seeing for herself that everything was in order. Miss Williams went about her task of uplifting the race with great gusto and an almost legendary determination, pacing the halls with her thick ruler ever at the ready.

Fannie Williams headed the school for thirty-three years; she continued teaching long after her formal retirement, and died in 1980 at the venerable age of ninety-seven.[3]

Many black schools in the pre-*Brown* era cultivated a strong ethos of racial pride. The Negro History movement, powered by the indefatigable and irascible Carter G. Woodson, found a natural constituency in black schoolteachers. In city schools, especially, teachers often succeeded in broadening the curriculum to include the study of the Negro. (They were careful, of course, to obtain the blessing of white superintendents—sometimes soothing away opposition by singing poignant renditions of the slave spirituals.) In New Orleans, a committee chaired by George S. Longe devised a program for Negro History Week that could be adapted to children of different ages. In addition to celebrating the achievements of black musicians, explorers, and athletes, they discussed the "economic status of the Negro in America." They learned, too, about writers like Dumas and Pushkin, and about Juan de Valladolid, a mayor of Seville in medieval times. By the 1940s, writes Carter G. Woodson's biographer, "Negro History Week celebrations became increasingly sophisticated and well attended." Even white politicians got in on the act, marking the annual event with proclamations of support.[4]

Angela Davis, who gained fame and notoriety in the 1960s as America's leading black Communist, attended Carrie A. Tuggle elementary school in Birmingham, Alabama. "Black identity was thrust upon us," she remembered. She learned about Frederick Douglass, Sojourner Truth and Harriet Tubman; at every assembly she thrilled to the words of James Weldon Johnson's song "Lift Every Voice and Sing"—the Negro national anthem. "I always sang the last phrases full blast: 'Facing the rising sun, till a new day is born, let us march on till victory is won!'" The notion that segregated black schools fostered feelings of racial inferiority—an argument endorsed by the Supreme Court in the *Brown* decision—flatly contradicted her own experience.[5]

At the same time, however, activists of the 1960s often criticized other aspects of their education. Angela Davis recalled that her teachers encouraged an ethos of competitive individualism ("Work hard and you will be rewarded") that ignored the racism that so often stymied ambition and nullified hard work. Andrew Young had similar memories, recalling an inordinate stress upon the outward appearance of middle-class respectability. Black teachers "seemed to believe that the path to freedom was to be found in manners and diction as much as intelligence and morality. It was an illusion." Moreover, the schools operated on the assumption that blacks would adapt to segregation, not challenge it. Tom Dent, who attended Gilbert Academy, one of the best private schools for blacks in the South, praised the excellence of his teachers but could not remember any of them ever suggesting the possibility of changing Jim Crow. Even at Howard University, the flagship of black education, "We never thought about intentionally violating the segregation laws."[6]

In fact, the Civil Rights movement sometimes prompted harsh judgments about black teachers. To people who were attacking segregation, black schools and colleges often seemed irrelevant or even harmful. After all, the uprising of 1955–65 sought to destroy Jim

Crow, not perpetuate it. The reports of civil rights organizations were peppered with complaints that black teachers failed to support the struggle against segregation. The NAACP was angered when black state colleges added "Jim Crow" graduate programs, even after the *Brown* decision; it was annoyed and frustrated by black teachers' lack of enthusiasm for school integration. In 1960, the student sit-in movement felt betrayed by the actions of black college presidents who bowed to segregationist politicians and expelled student leaders. When workers from the Student Nonviolent Coordinating Committee, the Congress of Racial Equality, and the Southern Christian Leadership Conference tried to organize local communities for open protest, they found little support among black teachers and routinely dismissed them as "the most Uncle Tom group around." Such criticisms suggest a fundamental contradiction between the institution-building efforts of black teachers during the Age of Segregation and the integrationist thrust of the Civil Rights movement.[7]

Some historians have underlined that contradiction, stressing the social and political conservatism of black teachers. In his study of South Carolina, for example, Idus A. Newby concluded that the Civil Rights movement took place despite, not because of, black schools and colleges, where "nothing was taught so assiduously as submission." More recently, Glenn Eskew has argued that the Civil Rights movement in Birmingham, Alabama, drew its support from only a handful of black ministers and a small group of predominantly working-class African Americans. When Fred L. Shuttlesworth and Martin Luther King Jr. launched the protests that rocked America in 1963, they found the bulk of the black middle class arrayed against them. When SCLC organizer James Bevel urged children at Parker High School to join in the demonstrations, principal R. C. Johnson locked the school gates in a futile effort to stop them.[8]

If schoolchildren learned nothing of the ideals of democracy and equality, if teachers were a professional clique of middle-class strivers, if colleges produced a snobbish elite that denigrated the masses as an unfortunate burden, if college presidents were primarily interested in feathering their own nests, and if educators generally urged blacks to accept white supremacy, then something had gone seriously wrong with black education. And if this were indeed the case, we would be entirely correct in viewing the Civil Rights movement as a repudiation of black leaders who lacked courage, vision and, sometimes, integrity.

But this, of course, cannot be the whole story. If it were, one would need to discount a substantial body of historical scholarship that explicitly links the black struggle for education with the black struggle for equality. As usual, it was Swedish social scientist Gunnar Myrdal who hit the nail on the head when he observed in *An American Dilemma* (1944) that "the long-range effect of the rising level of education in the Negro people goes in the direction of nourishing and strengthening the Negro protest." Twenty-three years later, in *A History of Negro Education in the South*, Henry Allen Bullock agreed that education, despite white efforts to curtail and control it, had functioned as the main lever "pushing forward the movement toward the complete emancipation of the Negro." Recent studies have arrived at the same conclusion. Black schools, writes James L. Leloudis, while inferior in many respects to white schools, served as "vital bridges between the freedom struggles of the late nineteenth century and those of the mid-twentieth." [9]

A few historians of the Civil Rights movement—Aldon Morris, Doug McAdam, Robert Norrell, William Chafe—have acknowledged the truth of these insights. Nevertheless, it is perhaps not so surprising that the burgeoning scholarship on the Civil Rights movement has neglected the extensive literature on black education. One reason is the problem of chronology. By focusing on the NAACP's attack on segregated schools and by dwelling on exciting boycotts and demonstrations, historians have underscored the distinctiveness of the period 1955–65, the "Montgomery-to-Selma" years. The milestones of the Civil Rights movement—*Brown*, the Montgomery bus boycott, the student sit-in movement—were so unexpected and dramatic that it seemed as if black southerners suddenly sloughed off their grudging acquiescence to segregation and rose up in defiant protest. The prominence of students and young people in the movement reinforced the idea that the torch of leadership had passed from one generation to another, a notion further encouraged by a wider cult of youth that emerged during the 1960s.[10]

A second reason for this neglect is that public school teachers were not especially prominent in the Civil Rights movement. In fact, writes John Dittmer, "As a group black teachers in the 1950s refused to take a stand, and the movement of the early 1960s passed them by." After the *Brown* decision, the focus of black leadership shifted from teachers to preachers.[11]

Both of these reasons, however, obscure important truths about the relationship between schooling and the struggle for racial equality. Despite real discontinuities between the periods before and after *Brown* and the Montgomery bus boycott, the Civil Rights movement built upon earlier struggles and had its roots in preceding decades. As we trace those roots it behooves us to cease viewing the Montgomery-to-Selma generation as uniquely heroic, uniquely idealistic, and uniquely endowed with political wisdom. Paying more attention to earlier periods, historians are finding that many different groups—workers, unions, liberal reformers, the Communist party—struggled against racial and economic oppression in the first half of the twentieth century.

So, too, did black teachers. In establishing schools and then struggling to raise standards, teachers helped to point the race in the direction of equality. Through patient, persistent advocacy they also persuaded influential whites—including many southerners—that public education should embody some measure of equality. Finally, if we examine the Civil Rights movement itself more carefully, we discover that teachers contributed to the NAACP's expansion in the South and helped to initiate the NAACP's attack on segregated education.

In developing my thesis, two problems must be admitted. The first is the difficulty of knowing what actually went on inside black schools and, in particular, how the children responded to teachers. The contemporary literature on education is enormous, but direct evidence from the classroom is surprisingly scarce. Nevertheless, from memoirs and oral histories, from school magazines and year-books, and from detailed surveys like the study of Louisiana's schools directed by Charles S. Johnson in 1940, one can piece together some idea of how black schools functioned in reality.

A second problem presents a more serious difficulty. Much of the sociological evidence about black schools derives from the 1930s, and the strongest theme of Depression-era reports is how awful they were. Investigators compiled a grim picture of classes still being held in dilapidated buildings, leaning at impossible angles, that lacked adequate lighting, heating, toilets, washing facilities, and even basic items like desks and tables. In such places a solitary teacher, usually a young woman with little more than a high-school education, struggled with classes of as many as seventy-five children spread over eight grades.[12]

In a one-teacher school in Macon County, Georgia, Arthur Raper asked a child named Booker T. Washington Williams for whom he had been named. Neither he nor any of the other pupils knew; not even the teacher knew. In 1939 Gunnar Myrdal "hardly believed his eyes and his ears" when he questioned students in a similar school. "No one could tell who the President of the United States was or even what the President was. . . . No one had heard of the NAACP." Asked about the Constitution of the United States, "All remained in solemn silence, until one bright boy helped us out, informing us that it was 'a newspaper in Atlanta.'"[13]

Lest one conclude that black children were clamming up in the presence of white visitors, black investigators recounted similar horror stories. Studying rural schools across the South, Charles S. Johnson encountered poorly prepared teachers, harsh punishments, rote learning, and a lifeless curriculum. Many lessons were exercises in confusion. Even if the building and the teacher were good, few children could leap over the chasm between the middle-class ideals of education and the realities of sharecropping or laboring. "Having no relation to life or its needs," concluded Johnson, "education has no meaning beyond the luxury of form." For many black children, therefore, education was a confusing, disturbing, alienating experience. Small wonder that so many left school at the earliest opportunity.[14]

Yet this relentlessly negative picture needs qualifying. First, many teachers endeavored to surmount apparently stupefying obstacles through sheer commitment. Dorothy Robinson recalled that she and others taught "with zeal and dedication . . . as though they felt a personal mandate to compensate for the areas of lack in the lives of their students." Inside the classroom, moreover, teachers enjoyed considerable freedom: white superintendents, especially in the rural South, rarely visited black schools. In east Texas, Robinson remembered, "I was a rather free agent and did just about what I wanted to do, as long as I did not ask for anything that would entail the expenditure of money."[15]

Rare descriptions of actual lessons can be quite revealing. In 1934 Estelle Massey Riddle, president of the National Association of Colored Graduate Nurses, observed classes in a rural Louisiana school as part of a study sponsored by the Rosenwald Fund. In a history lesson, the teacher asked, "Why do we have this period of Reformation? What caused Christianity to stand, brave men or scary men? How can we reform our community rights here in Mineral Springs?" According to Riddle's notes, "A good discussion followed." The teacher then asked his class to compare Charlemagne and Huey Long. Did Charlemagne have the rich people with him? Did Governor Long have the rich people with him? What had Huey Long done for the poor people of Louisiana? "Paved highways and free textbooks," chorused the children. A skeptic might see this Socratic dialogue as evidence that teachers in Louisiana felt obliged to curry favor with a spoils-ridden, authoritarian political machine. But Riddle, who was not easily fooled, viewed it as an effective lesson that encouraged students to think about citizenship. The children had asked "good thought-provoking questions," she noted, and were "enthusiastic and spontaneous." [16]

Second, the quality of teaching in black schools steadily improved after 1920. As the power of state education bureaucracies increased, the habit of treating teaching posts as a form of patronage declined. State officials progressively raised the requirements for teacher certification, encouraging or requiring teachers to attend summer institutes, and made would-be teachers jump over higher and higher educational hurdles. A twelfth-grade education no longer guaranteed a teaching job: some college training was expected. In 1930, only 12 percent of black teachers were college graduates. Ten years later, the proportion was 35 percent; by 1952 it stood at 72 percent. [17]

Improvements in black schools were especially marked in the city high schools, which 1930s investigators tended to neglect. Often described as "training schools" or "industrial high schools," black secondary schools were designed to train teachers on the cheap and to slot blacks into lower occupations that would insulate whites from competition. Blacks, however, resisted efforts to concentrate upon manual trades because, as one expert noted in 1937, to "depart from a purely academic curriculum would be to admit of racial inferiority." Whites, moreover, refused to fund the workshops and equipment that would have enabled these schools to provide proper vocational training. Black high schools, therefore, quickly became carbon copies—albeit less well-funded—of white high schools. At Booker T. Washington High School in Houston, for example, the faculty of 1928 included three math teachers, two English teachers, two history teachers, two Latin teachers, a biology teacher, a science teacher, and a civics teacher. There were two home economics teachers, but only one person taught "industrial arts." In many cities, it is true, whites refused to countenance black public high schools. But after 1930 such opposition gradually diminished, and after 1940 rapidly so. [18]

Foundation officials like Thomas Jesse Jones of the Phelps-Stokes Fund deplored the increase in time devoted to "conventional book knowledge" in black schools and complained that even rural schools neglected to teach agriculture. However, blacks themselves knew better. By the 1930s cotton, once a corpulent King, had become a starving beggar with protruding ribs and spindly legs, surviving mainly on federal handouts. Agriculture was a dead end, and blacks increasingly rejected the notion that their children should be educated to stay on the farm. A Rosenwald Fund report on South Carolina State College revealed the realism of black ambitions and the obsolescence of white educational thinking. The report criticized the desultory character of the college's agricultural teaching, and complained that the engineering department had started a course in, of all things, air-conditioning—which it dismissed as irrelevant to the needs of the South! [19]

The reality was that blacks perceived a high school education as a means of escaping the poverty, cultural isolation, and political tyranny of the southern countryside. A 1940 survey of high school students in Louisiana revealed that boys aspired to be teachers, doctors, aviators, mail clerks, ministers, carpenters, and lawyers; girls wanted to be teachers, nurses, seamstresses, beauticians, stenographers, and musicians. Anything but farmers. Even among the sons of farmers, a mere 8 percent expressed any desire to follow in their fathers' footsteps. Even at the black land-grant colleges, only about 10 percent of students took courses in agriculture, and even fewer actually returned to farming. The overwhelming majority, in fact, became teachers. [20]

Most of those teachers were women. By 1930 women made up at least three-quarters of the South's black teaching force, and in some states the proportion was much higher. Counting the teachers in 196 Louisiana schools, Charles Johnson found 74 men and 390 women. Of the 132 teachers in the small elementary schools, only 7 were men. Among college-trained teachers, men were sometimes invisible. When Straight University in New Orleans graduated its first teachers in 1892, all 7 were women. Fifty-two years later, at Jackson State College in Mississippi, the first 29 graduate teachers included no men. [21]

That women made up the vast majority of black teachers should not surprise us: the feminization of America's teaching profession was universal, just as marked among white teachers as black. Yet the relative paucity of black male teachers may well have had additional significance. Black women were often preferred by white school boards and education officials, who saw them as more pliable and accommodating than black men. As James Leloudis has suggested, white officials "felt more at ease with black women and viewed them as less of a political liability."[22]

Yet appearances could serve more than one purpose. By eschewing assertive or confrontational behavior, women teachers were often adept at manipulating white officials to their advantage—and to the advantage of their community. Hortense Powdermaker was astonished to see how a college-educated Jeanes teacher in Sunflower County, Mississippi, "a strong self-respecting person," transformed herself into "the essence of meekness" in front of her white superintendent. Afterward, with a cynical chuckle, the teacher explained to the anthropologist how by "acting proper" she secured books, equipment, playgrounds, and better wages for black teachers. Blacks understood these facts of life. "She was admired and liked by all the Negroes," Powdermaker recalled. Such behavior, Glenda Gilmore has argued, represented more than bowing and scraping to white paternalism. After disfranchisement, black women became "spokespeople for and motivators of black citizens," and the "deep camouflage of their leadership style—their womanhood—helped them remain invisible as they worked toward political ends." Slowly and subtly, black women bent paternalism into interracialism, a relationship that implied mutual respect and hinted at equality."[23]

Here, perhaps, we can throw light upon a paradox of the Civil Rights movement that has never been satisfactorily explained: although the movement displayed an overwhelmingly male leadership, women probably comprised a majority of its most active supporters. Why this disparity? Perhaps the Civil Rights movement reproduced the pattern of the black church, in which the ministers were men while most of the active church members were women. Perhaps women were more accustomed to participating in community activities generally, through involvement in social clubs, voluntary work, and kinship networks. Perhaps the philosophy of nonviolence propounded by SCLC, SNCC, and CORE deterred some men from joining demonstrations that required them to turn the other cheek in an "unmanly" fashion. Perhaps the men who led the movement shared "male chauvinist" prejudices that obstructed the inclusion of women.

Yet education might also have a bearing on the question. Black women, Hortense Powdermaker noted, found it easier to sustain faith in education because they remained more hopeful about the future generally. She speculated that their nurturing role as mothers made women, almost necessarily, more sanguine. "The children carry them ahead into a future where more may be possible; and the future seems more promising, more important, more worth struggling for, because of the children." This is why, perhaps, in the autobiographies of prominent black figures as well as in the memories of more humble folk, mothers loom so large in encouraging children to attend school. The harsh facts of morbidity also had something to do with this: Ambrose Caliver's 1933 study of black college students revealed that a staggering 27 percent were fatherless through death while only 16 percent had lost their mothers.[24]

Just as mothers usually had more formal education than fathers, so daughters were likely to go further in their education than sons. Whether daughters received more parental encouragement than sons is difficult to establish. In the rural South, certainly, the labor of sons was more vital to raising cotton and other life-sustaining crops; it mattered less if daughters, especially the younger ones, left the fields to attend school. Yet in the towns as well, more girls than boys attended school, a disproportion that increased as children grew older. By grades eight to eleven, according to Charles Johnson's

1940 survey of Louisiana, girls outnumbered boys by two to one. By then, girls also comprised a majority of black college students and were more likely to graduate.[25]

What I am suggesting is that women's strong commitment to education encouraged support for, and participation in, the Civil Rights movement. The improvement of educational opportunities was a central concern of the movement, and women were prominent in efforts to integrate the South's schools. Perhaps, in addition, their faith in education made women more sympathetic to the basic ethos of the Civil Rights movement, which was rooted in optimism and idealism. Finally, because women were better educated than men, they might have been more inclined to engage in political activism.

As Stephanie Shaw argues in her study of black women professionals, many female teachers had a strong sense of vocation, displaying hope, self-confidence, and dedication to service. They learned those values from their own families and teachers. Through teaching, writes Shaw, these educated women believed they could "'uplift' the race, develop the community, gain for it the more equitable place in society it deserved, while creating for themselves important positions of leadership." When the *Brown* decision encouraged black southerners to openly challenge white supremacy, this vision of community development helped to create and sustain the Civil Rights movement.[26]

In the 1920s and 1930s, when open protest against white supremacy was rare and dangerous, teachers still had to be extraordinarily resourceful in order to improve schools. A. C. Facin, who headed Mineral Springs School in Ouchita Parish, Louisiana, typified the kind of teacher who, in Booker T. Washington's words, "go into lonely desolate districts with little hope of getting salaries, where there are little personal comforts or the evidence of living, and give themselves in this beautiful manner to the uplift of our people." During his ten years as principal, Facin leveled the site for the new three-teacher Rosenwald school, added a home economics room, built his own house, organized canning clubs, and developed a school farm that included a grist mill and vehicle repair shop. In 1933 the school made $118 from the sale of two bales of cotton: enough to pay for a second-hand piano, fix broken windows, and replace missing door knobs. In his early days Facin contended against jealousy, lack of co-operation, and threats from parents who were angered by the corporal punishment Facin inflicted on their children. Faced with pressures that might have destroyed his effectiveness, Facin enlisted the aid of the local mail rider, "one mean white man," to "sort out" the families who had threatened him.[27] The fact that Facin appealed to a white person to intercede for him exemplified the double-edged nature of teachers' leadership in this period. Teachers still practiced accommodationism—also called "toadying" or "bowing and scraping"—in dealing with whites.

When a black high school principal "wanted to develop a band or an athletic team he exploited local pride," wrote Tuskegee sociologist Lewis W. Jones. "His appeal for support . . . was that the good white people of Sandusky couldn't afford to let those of neighboring Belltown provide better for their Negro school." Many a principal still exploited that old standby, the Negro spiritual. Arthur Harold Parker, who created the most famous black high school in the South, assiduously cultivated Birmingham's superintendent, John Herbert Phillips, who, like many other whites, could be moved to tears by hearing "those plaintive, tuneful and soul stirring melodies." On one occasion, Parker recalled, Phillips lamented that if the high school got an orchestra instructor, the young people might forget the slave songs. "You will get an instructor of orchestra on one condition," the superintendent promised, "and that is that you will always sing these old songs."[28]

By the Second World War, however, black teachers were no longer so willing to pursue piecemeal gains in a pragmatic compromise with white supremacy. Quantitative improvements, even if they brought better schools and higher academic standards, would not translate into economic and political gains if they failed to narrow the gap with white schools. Teachers wanted to close that gap completely, and in the 1930s they made equal opportunity their explicit goal.

At state and national levels, teachers formed professional organizations that openly campaigned for equality. The most important of these, the American Teachers Association, founded in 1904, documented the disparities between black and white schools, exposed racism in textbooks and motion pictures, promoted Negro history, lobbied the federal government, and sought recognition from the lily-white National Education Association. In 1930 teachers initiated a tenacious campaign—which did not bear fruit until the 1960s—to have black high schools and colleges accredited on precisely the same basis as white institutions. The *Journal of Negro Education* and the *Quarterly Journal of Higher Education for Negroes*, both launched in the 1930s, produced top quality research and sponsored political discussions.[29]

To black students like Andrew Young, who years later lamented the political passivity of his teachers, most of this extracurricular work would have been invisible. Yet teachers like Fannie Williams, the redoubtable principal of Valena C. Jones school, were indefatigable in their service to organizations like the ATA. Yes, they preached the necessity of individual achievement, but they also worked collectively to promote equal opportunity for all. If teachers shied away from discussing, let alone challenging, segregation, that is understandable. Jim Crow was the law of the land, and in 1940 it seemed immovable. Yet teachers did encourage their students to consider social and political issues, and not merely through the teaching of Negro history. Fannie Williams, for example, persuaded a stream of nationally known figures to visit Valena C. Jones: in 1938–39 alone her students heard Jesse Owens, Dale Carnegie, and Rev. Marshall Shepherd, a black politician from Philadelphia who argued that blacks in the South would soon be voting. In the same year students debated a motion that "Negro colleges and universities should stress technological rather than cultural training." The motion went down to a resounding defeat.[30]

By 1940 black teachers were winning the argument about equality of opportunity. They were helped, of course, by the decline of scientific racism, a process accelerated by the Second World War. They were assisted by the New Deal, which offered help for the common man, redefined freedom in expansive terms, and celebrated democracy—an idea that had languished for half a century—with infectious enthusiasm. And teachers also found sympathetic allies in southern liberals who, inspired by Roosevelt's concern for the South's economic problems, viewed mass poverty among the black population as a brake upon the region's development. Throughout the South, in bold statements of democratic idealism, white education officials proclaimed a new egalitarianism that embraced black people with generosity. Louisiana: "Democracy is free from prejudice. Educating *all* the people is important." Georgia: "The democratic society is a society in which people are working together in the attempt to secure a genuine and full opportunity." Tennessee: "Every child . . . is entitled to an equal educational opportunity."[31]

The rhetoric of southern liberals, however, represented hope rather than reality. With blacks still disfranchised, the only inducement for county superintendents to improve black schools was their own conscience—and Christian virtue had to contend with the skepticism, indifference, and outright hostility of white voters. John C. Dixon, Georgia's director of Negro education, described the result: "Year after year, we see an increase in the total expenditure of public money on education in the South. Year after year, also, there is a wider gap in the relative amounts spent on educating white children and Negro children." All the evidence suggested that whites in the South would not actually implement equality of educational opportunity. As a committee of black teachers concluded in 1945, changing public sentiment was "entirely too big a task for Negro school people alone."[32]

Enter the NAACP. In the mid-1930s the association initiated law suits that challenged racial discrimination in the public schools and colleges of the South. Devised and prosecuted by Charles H. Houston and Thurgood Marshall, the NAACP's strategy targeted two areas where discrimination was flagrant, easy to document, and difficult to justify: the absence of graduate education for blacks and the grossly inferior salaries paid to black schoolteachers. These were, in fact, the opening salvos of a legal assault on Jim Crow that in 1954 yielded the NAACP's most famous victory, *Brown v. Board of Education.* The NAACP considered the backing of black teachers vital to the success of this campaign.

NAACP leaders complained, in private, that black teachers offered only timid and halfhearted support. Yet the enormity of backing the NAACP's strategy can hardly be overestimated. Teachers risked alienating the northern philanthropic foundations, which disapproved of the NAACP's confrontational tactics. They were being asked to reject the paternalism of white state officials who were, by and large, sincere advocates of black education. They had to align with a New York–based organization that was feared and detested by southern whites. Above all, the NAACP required teachers to sue their employers in federal court, and plaintiffs were putting their jobs on the line. It is not surprising that black teachers, initially at least, were divided about the wisdom of throwing their lot in with the NAACP.[33]

The situation in Georgia was typical. For years, the state association of black teachers, the GTEA, had worked hand in glove with the white directors of Negro education. In the trough of the Great Depression, John C. Dixon helped to save the GTEA from bankruptcy. His successor, Robert L. Cousins, helped the GTEA to plan its meetings and conduct its internal affairs. Black teachers not only had friends in these men, but also shared a common enemy in the person of Gene Talmadge, an unscrupulous demagogue and race-baiter. In 1940 Talmadge plunged education into the maelstrom of racial politics when he dismissed Walter Cocking, dean of education at the University of Georgia, and Marvin S. Pittman, president of Georgia Teachers College, for being too sympathetic to blacks. Talmadge even attacked the Rosenwald Fund, describing it as "Jew money for niggers."

It was not surprising, therefore, that when Robert Cousins proposed to equalize teachers salaries in stages, over ten years, the GTEA agreed to forgo litigation: any intervention by the NAACP would only play into Talmadge's hands in the 1942 gubernatorial election. The decision elicited a blistering riposte from Walter Chivers, a sociology professor at Morehouse College—and incidentally, one of Martin Luther King Jr.'s favorite teachers—who attacked the GTEA's "misleadership" as an unrepresentative clique from south Georgia. "What are the Negro teachers in Georgia afraid of anyway? . . . Do [they] mean to continue teaching in inadequate school buildings, working for starvation wages?" An insurgent faction of NAACP supporters insisted on going to court.[34]

Struggles for control of the state teachers associations took place throughout the South, with the pro-NAACP forces denouncing the conservatives as Uncle Toms, stool pigeons, pimps, appeasers, and "'Yes, yes,' whitefolks men." The NAACP supporters emerged victorious—even in Mississippi—leading to a battery of equalization suits. Irate school boards fired most of the plaintiffs, as well as several teachers' leaders, and devised "merit" systems in an effort to continue paying black teachers less. Still, although some discrimination persisted, by the late 1940s the litigation had largely succeeded.

Although not terribly dramatic, the salaries campaign was an important victory. It put money into teachers' pockets, established crucial legal precedents, and forged an alliance between black teachers and the NAACP. In Louisiana, North Carolina, and elsewhere, the black teachers associations financed the NAACP's lawsuits in the field of education. In addition, for every dollar that the American Teachers Association received in membership dues, it gave ten cents to the NAACP Legal Defense and Educational Fund—the "Ink Fund" for short—headed by Thurgood Marshall. Above all, the campaign represented a psychological turning point for many participants. "It was my first effort in social action challenging the status quo," recalled South Carolina teacher Septima Clark, "the first time I had worked *against* people directing a system for which I was working."[35]

When the NAACP won its first courtroom victories against racial discrimination in education, black teachers in the South finally gained some bargaining power. Alarmed by the prospect of court-ordered integration, governors appointed commissions to study the situation. Helped by tax revenues generated by the postwar economic boom, state legislatures appropriated substantial sums to replace wooden schools with brick buildings and build black high schools where none had existed before. In Louisiana, the per capita sum allocated to black children increased from $16 in 1940 to $116 in 1955, from 24 percent of the amount spent on white children to 72 percent. South Carolina earmarked a $75 million bond issue and a 3 percent sales tax for equalizing black schools. In 1950 even Mississippi started an ambitious schoolbuilding program. Black colleges also gained. North Carolina State saw its budget grow from $23,000 in 1934 to $171,000 ten years later. Louisiana gave Southern University a law school. Florida gave A & M graduate programs in pharmacy, nursing, and education. Texas finally gave its black citizens a university—two in fact.[36]

An exchange within the Governor's Committee on Higher Education for Negroes in Alabama, appointed by James "Big Jim" Folsom in 1949, revealed the determination of black teachers to press the issue of equality. White members of the committee argued that "the ultimate goal is providing adequate education for Negroes." The blacks contended that "adequate" meant "equal." Whites demurred: "I would not say equal," said one; "There is no way to get your complete equality," agreed another. But H. C. Trenholm of Alabama State College refused to concede the argument. "But the law says available to one should be available to all. . . . The State has a moral obligation to provide it in some way."[37]

The strategy of equalization, however, contained a fundamental weakness. Even if—and that was a very big "if"—whites improved black schools and colleges to a point where they resembled white facilities, they still intended to maintain a racial division of labor in the economy. Equality of educational opportunity was a cruel deception in a society organized around the principle of white supremacy.

The opinions of the men who ran public schools at the local level, the county superintendents, were far more indicative of white opinion than the liberal views of unelected state agents. A 1930 survey indicated that three-quarters of North Carolina's superintendents believed that "the average Negro pupil does not have as much capacity to learn as the average white pupil." Not much had changed by 1940. "It was silly to teach French and similar subjects to colored people," thought the superintendent of McDowell County. The man from Salisbury complained that black children "were more interested in preparing themselves for so-called 'white collar' jobs than for any kind of manual labor." Blacks only wanted school buses, added the superintendent of Franklin County, "as a means of getting away from the farms." One Negro father wanted his daughter to be a stenographer—"a most unholy ambition." Blacks desired "impractical and useless courses," declared the official from High Point, "simply because they were offered in the white high schools."[38]

The black high schools and colleges were, in effect, educating black youth for jobs monopolized by whites. Indeed, even those jobs traditionally occupied by blacks were diminishing: during the 1920s and 1930s whites had displaced many black craftsmen and skilled workers, pushing blacks further down the economic ladder. With the continuing decline of southern agriculture, blacks faced economic disaster. In 1938 one of the South's leading white educators warned that "If we train Negroes to live a life which human society forbids them to live after we have educated them . . . I should expect such educated persons to become Bolshevists." Actually, few did: they became teachers and ministers, joined labor unions, joined the NAACP, moved to the cities, and quit the South in droves.[39]

When the Second World War invigorated the economy, blacks demanded access to well-paid jobs in the defense industries. The federal government supported them—responding to the threat of A. Philip Randolph's "March on Washington"—by creating the Fair Employment Practices Committee. Yet whites continued to oppose the training and recruitment of skilled black workers with a determination that sometimes spilled over into violence. Southern shipyards, for example, were crying out for skilled workers, but blacks found themselves barred from welding jobs. When the NAACP branch in New Iberia, Louisiana, obtained a welding class after the FEPC's intervention, the sheriff and the school superintendent had the black leaders run out of town. In Mobile, the introduction of a dozen black welders sparked rioting among white shipyard workers. The government's policy of nondiscrimination proved unenforceable, and southern congressmen succeeded in abolishing the FEPC in 1946. The doors of southern industry had opened a crack but then closed again.[40]

In 1934 the president of the North Carolina black teachers association asked, "Is it to be the policy to confine Negroes to certain occupations . . . or is it to be the American policy to both allow and encourage their participation in all of the occupational phases of the national life?" Ten years later the answer was clear: as far as whites were concerned, the Negro's economic status after the war would be pretty much what it had been before the war. A 1942 study of Louisiana's schools recommended that blacks be educated for life "as a plantation worker, as a tenant farmer, as a farm owner, as a domestic servant, as a laborer . . . and as a professional man or woman rendering service to his own race." A state education official put matters more bluntly: blacks had an "unrealistic outlook" and wanted to "get as far away as possible from anything that smacks of labor and work." The vast majority were farmers and laborers, and "the vast majority of their children will follow similar occupations."[41]

Separate-but-equal was a myth because segregation was imposed by whites to maintain white supremacy. The NAACP knew this and had long regarded equalization as a means to an end, not an end in itself. Segregation-by-law was entirely inconsistent with the NAACP's philosophy, which condemned it as being "economically unsound" and for "work[ing] against the development of mutual respect and understanding." As Thurgood Marshall told black teachers in 1945, the NAACP calculated that forcing states to ensure absolute equality would make segregation so expensive as to be unsustainable. But in 1950 Marshall decided that the time was ripe to attack segregation head-on, challenging the legal principle itself. It was a strategic decision to attack Jim Crow at what appeared to be its most vulnerable point.[42]

Nobody knew, however, precisely what integration would entail and what its ultimate shape would be. It was a leap in the dark. W. E. B. Du Bois argued that "most Negroes would prefer a good school with properly paid colored teachers, to forcing children into white schools which met them with injustice and discouraged their efforts to progress." And he predicted that "if any outside power forced white and colored children in the same schools, the result would be turmoil and uprising as would utterly nullify the process of education." Du Bois was correct on the second point, and probably right about the first. Among blacks in the South, the NAACP's new policy produced strong, if mostly silent, misgivings.[43]

Black teachers had particular worries, because integration—as whites were quick to point out—would involve shutting down black schools, phasing out black colleges, and abolishing thousands of jobs. The integration of the University of Louisville in 1950, which led to the closure of Louisville Municipal College and the dismissal of five of its six black teachers, was not a happy precedent. The NAACP promised to do everything within its power to prevent teachers from being intimidated and dismissed. In 1955 it created the Department of Teacher Information and Security. Its head, John W. Davis, the former president of West Virginia State College, understood the vulnerability of black teachers. Lacking tenure, they were at the mercy of local school boards. For a black teacher, moreover, dismissal represented economic calamity. White teachers had a variety of white-collar career options; black teachers did not.[44]

A year after the *Brown* decision, southern politicians began turning the screws on black public school teachers. In Georgia, state attorney general Eugene Cook branded the NAACP a Communist organization and advised that any teacher supporting it should be fired. In Albany, the superintendent of schools summoned black teachers and harangued them on the evils of the NAACP. In one Georgia county every teacher was handed a pro-segregation petition, to be returned with the signatures of black parents before their contracts were renewed. In Virginia, a state law authorized school boards to dismiss teachers consequent to any "decrease in attendance or enrollment." In 1956 state officials in the South launched a concerted attack upon the NAACP that specifically targeted black teachers. New laws forbade them to advocate integration and required them to resign from the association. A few individuals, like Septima Clark of Charleston, resisted. The entire staff of one South Carolina school quit in protest. The majority of teachers, however, chose to retain their jobs by resigning from the NAACP.[45]

Many in the NAACP were disgusted that teachers, who comprised the backbone of many branches, quit the organization en masse. But teachers were frightened, and they felt abandoned. They were abandoned by the federal government, which sat back and allowed the southern states to stifle freedom of association; abandoned by the National Education Association, which for years failed to endorse the *Brown* decision and ignored the plight of black teachers in the South; abandoned even by the NAACP, which invited black teachers to attack segregation from the trenches without the benefit of infantry, artillery, or air support. Moreover, the NAACP's basic outlook was that the career interests of black educators were less important than the elimination of segregated schools. Before the *Brown* decision, Fred Patterson had warned that black teachers would not greet integration with "a wave of enthusiasm." After *Brown*, recalled NAACP lawyer Constance Baker Motley, black teachers became "a major foe of school desegregation."[46]

Motley's judgment was an oversimplification. Even in the darkest days of massive resistance, black teachers organizations continued to cooperate with the NAACP. And in the 1960s, after acrimonious debate, those organizations voted themselves out of existence and merged with the white teachers. The fact is that school integration divided black teachers because it divided the black community at large.[47]

Moreover, widespread disappointment over the results of integration provided a useful corrective to the NAACP's harsh judgments on black teachers. In many cities, the public schools integrated only to resegregate. Even when black and white children attend the same schools, the educational benefits have proved elusive. Moreover, integration came at a high price; it closed thousands of schools that blacks had built at great personal sacrifice and that had provided vital community cohesion. Many have wondered whether integration merited that cost. "What, exactly, was wrong with the old black public schools that for years served their constituencies so well despite the deprivations and the isolation of segregation?" asked Tom Dent shortly before his death. "There is inescapable irony in the fact that those older schools provided much of what is lacking in today's postsegregation schools: the desperately needed psychological support . . .[and] a sense of the historical continuity of the educational experience of their race through the existence of the school itself."[48]

Some segregated black schools were indeed excellent, and their closure was a great loss. Edmund Jefferson Oliver headed Fairfield Industrial High School in Alabama for forty-three years. Administering corporal punishment freely but resorting to expulsion on only twenty occasions, he inculcated the old-fashioned virtues of Christian morality in a forthright manner that would be impermissible today. Traveling far and wide to recruit the best teachers and seeing that they taught within their fields, Oliver oversaw a disciplined but caring school that instilled great loyalty in the children who passed through it. "If necessary," he boasted, "I can get in touch with a thousand of the 3,162 graduates within ninety days."[49]

There were schools like Oliver's throughout the South, where dedicated principals and devoted teachers refused to let segregation undermine their sense of vocation. They communicated their faith in the possibilities of education to more children and more parents than circumstances should have warranted. They also insisted upon personal responsibility and high moral standards. In 1979, anticipating a "grand reunion" of graduates of Ballard Normal School in Macon, Eldred Davis sorrowfully reflected that "not one of the black schools of my youth now exists as such—Pleasant Hill, Ballard Normal, Georgia State. I very biasedly feel that the race and the world are diminished by their absence and the knowledge and values they so effectively transmitted." [50]

We must not romanticize the black schools of the pre-integration era. As Tom Dent conceded, he knew only the best of them; many were truly awful. Moreover, the situation of black teachers not only militated against overt involvement in the Civil Rights movement but also caused some teachers to question the movement itself. When a dozen students at Fairfield School took part in one of Martin Luther King's marches, Edmund Oliver suspended them. "Two or three of the self-styled leaders of the community called a meeting at the school," he recalled with distaste, "for the purpose of getting the students back in school without receiving any kind of punishment." To Oliver, such actions smacked of irresponsibility and threatened to undermine the basic glue, discipline, that held his school together. To the movement, however, such concerns were trivial: men like Oliver were spitting against the wind of history.[51]

Despite the shortcomings of integration, no amount of historical revisionism can negate the significance of the *Brown* decision in undermining the foundations of white supremacy. The central role of Jim Crow laws in the subordination of black southerners made an attack on segregated schools unavoidable. *Plessy v. Ferguson* had to be destroyed—even if black teachers, black schools, and black communities paid a heavy price. NAACP lawyer William Ming stated the matter with cruel honesty: "There are fatalities in all social change." [52]

In 1944 Gunnar Myrdal noted that for black teachers in the South "the temptation to sell out the group and to look out for his own petty interest is great." There were certainly some teachers for whom the strategy of "double agent," to use Glenda Gilmore's simile, led to corruption and betrayal. Their duplicity is documented in the recently opened files of the Mississippi State Sovereignty Commission, which reveal that some principals informed on the NAACP.[53]

Yet most black teachers did not allow the demands of accommodationism to vitiate their integrity or obscure their larger purpose. Vanessa Siddle Walker's fine history of a black high school in North Carolina concludes that teachers struggled to improve black education within a political system anchored on black disfranchisement, motivating students to learn and even excel and opposing the racist stereotypes that constantly threatened to sap black self-respect. The incremental gains they achieved did not destroy white supremacy; by the 1960s they seemed pathetically inadequate. Yet as James D. Anderson has insisted, "There was nothing naive about a belief in learning and self-improvement as a means to individual and collective dignity. It was not the end of their struggle for freedom and justice; only a means toward that end."[54] During the grim years of Jim Crow black teachers had to work within the confines of segregation and were unable to furnish overt political leadership. Yet in resisting the basic ideas of white supremacy—racism and inequality—they helped to undermine the Jim Crow regime. By insisting upon the sanctity of knowledge and the innate humanity of black children, they performed political work of the most far-reaching kind.

Notes

Liberation or Collaboration?

1 Annie W. Day to Charles N. Hunter, March 18, 1887; Louise S. Dorr to Hunter, October 15, 1887, box 1, Charles N. Hunter Papers, Perkins Library, Duke University; Minutes of the Seventh Annual Session of the Alabama State Teachers Association, Selma, April 11–13, 1888, box 30A, H. C. Trenholm Papers, Moorland-Spingarn Library, Howard University.

2 For positive appraisals of the role of education in the history of black southerners, see Henry Allen Bullock, *A History of Negro Education in the South: From 1619 to the Present* (Cambridge: Harvard University Press, 1967), vii–ix; James L. Leloudis, *Schooling the New South: Pedagogy, Self, and Society in North Carolina, 1880–1920* (Chapel Hill: University of North Carolina Press), 223; Michael R. Heintze, *Private Black Colleges in Texas, 1865–1954* (College Station: Texas A&M University Press, 1985), 11–13, 170; James M. McPherson, *The Abolitionist Legacy: From Reconstruction to the NAACP* (Princeton: Princeton University Press, 1975, 1995), 393; William Preston Vaughan, *Schools for All: The Blacks and Public Education in the South, 1865–1877* (Lexington: University Press of Kentucky, 1977); Robert C. Morris, *Reading, 'Riting, and Reconstruction: The Education of Freedmen in the South, 1861–1870* (Chicago: University of Chicago Press, 1982); Jacqueline Jones, *Soldiers of Light and Love: Northern Teachers and Georgia Blacks, 1865–1875* (Athens: University of Georgia Press, 1980, 1992); Joe M. Richardson, *Christian Reconstruction: The American Missionary Association and Southern Blacks, 1861–1890* (Athens: University of Georgia Press, 1986); James D. Anderson, *The Education of Blacks in the South 1860–1935* (Chapel Hill: University of North Carolina Press, 1988), 279–85.

3 Education in the South, until quite recently, was a confusing patchwork of public and private; local variations were the rule, not the exception; distinctions between elementary, secondary, and higher were vague.

4 E. Franklin Frazier, *The Negro Family in the United States* (Chicago: Uni-

versity of Chicago Press, 1966), 190–205; Minutes of the Seventh Annual Session of the Alabama State Teachers Association, Selma, April 11–13, 1888; Minutes of the Eighth Annual Session of the Alabama State Teachers Association, Selma, April 10–12, 1889, box 30A, H. C. Trenholm Papers.

5 Willard Range, *The Rise and Progress of Negro Colleges in Georgia, 1865–1949* (Athens: University of Georgia Press, 1951), 4; Betty Mansfield, "That Fateful Class: Black Teachers of Virginia's Freedmen, 1861–1882," Ph.D. diss., Catholic University of America, 1980, 1–52; Anderson, *Education of Blacks*, 281–85; Thomas L. Webber, *Deep Like the Rivers: Education in the Slave Quarters, 1831–1865* (New York: Norton, 1978); Morris, *Reading, 'Riting, and Reconstruction*, 95–96.

6 Mansfield, "That Fateful Class," 80–102, 258; Ronald Butchart, *Northern Schools, Southern Blacks, and Reconstruction, 1862–1875* (Westport CT: Greenwood Press, 1980), 169–72; Jones, *Soldiers of Light and Love*, 73; Range, *Rise and Progress of Negro Colleges*, 14; James D. Anderson, "Ex-Slaves and the Rise of Universal Education in the New South, 1860–1880," in Ronald K. Goodenow and Arthur O. White, eds., *Education and the Rise of the New South* (Boston: G. K. Hall, 1981), 1–10; Vaughan, *Schools for All*, 14–15; Morris, *Reading, 'Riting, and Reconstruction*, 91.

7 Morris, *Reading, 'Riting, and Reconstruction*, 103–8; John H. Haley, *Charles N. Hunter and Race Relations in North Carolina* (Chapel Hill: University of North Carolina Press, 1987), 34, 57; Nathan C. Newbold, *Five North Carolina Negro Educators* (Chapel Hill: University of North Carolina Press, 1939), 123–34; Elizabeth Ross Haynes, *Unsung Heroes; The Black Boy of Atlanta; "Negroes in Domestic Service in the United States"* (New York: G. K. Hall, 1952, 1997), 387–402; Minutes of the Seventh Annual Session of the Alabama State Teachers Association, Selma, April 11–12, 1888; Minutes of the Eighth Annual Session of the Alabama State Teachers Association, Selma, April 10–12, 1889; S. G. Atkins to Charles N. Hunter, September 30, 1886, Charles N. Hunter Papers, Perkins Library, Duke University.

8 W. E. B. Du Bois and August Granville Dill, *The College-Bred Negro American* (Atlanta: Atlanta University Press, 1910; reprint, New York: Arno Press, 1968), 66; U.S. Bureau of the Census, *The Social and Economic Status of the Black Population in the United States: An Historical View*,

1790–1978 (Washington DC: U.S. Government Printing Office, 1978), 76.

9   Anderson, *Education of Blacks*, 158–85; Edwin R. Embree, *Julius Rosenwald Fund: A Review to June 30, 1928* (Chicago: Julius Rosenwald Fund, 1928), 26; Nathan C. Newbold, "Negro Education" [1930], box 1, Special Subject Files, Department of Public Instruction, North Carolina Division of Archives and History. Blacks provided 17 percent of the money to build Rosenwald Schools, the Rosenwald Fund itself only 15 percent. The rest came from tax funds (64 percent) and "white friends" (4 percent).

10   "Washington Parish," box 225, folder 1, Charles S. Johnson Papers, Fisk University, Nashville; Horace Mann Bond and Julia W. Bond, "A Description of Washington Parish" [1934], part 2, microfilm reel 30, Horace Mann Bond Papers, Duke University.

11   Robinson, *The Bell Rings at Four: A Black Teacher's Chronicle of Change* (Austin: Madrona Press, 1978), 22–23; Charles N. Hunter, "East Raleigh School Second Session, 1879–1880" [1930], box 1, Hunter Papers; Leloudis, *Schooling the New South*, 206.

12   "Report of Two or More Teachers Group, Regular Teachers Meeting, Jackson, Tennessee," January 15, 1938, reel 279, folder 2, Department of Education Records, Record Group 92, Tennessee State Archives, Nashville; Robinson, *The Bell Rings at Four*, 14, 45.

13   Hortense Powdermaker, *After Freedom: A Cultural Study in the Deep South* (New York: Athenaeum, 1939, 1969), 310; Charles S. Johnson, *The Negro Public Schools: A Social and Educational Survey* (Baton Rouge: Louisiana Educational Survey Commission, 1942), 30.

14   Butchart, *Northern Schools, Southern Blacks, and Reconstruction*, 173.

15   Jones, *Soldiers of Light and Love*, 73–74; Mansfield, "That Fateful Class," 116; William Lowery to D. Burt, November 26, 1866, microfilm reel 47, Freedmen's Bureau Papers, Tennessee State Archives, Nashville; Josephine Price Sherrill, "A Negro School-Master of the 1870s," *Journal of Negro Education* 30 (spring 1961), 168.

16   Mansfield, "That Fateful Class," 341–44; Howard N. Rabinowitz, "Half a Loaf: The Shift from White to Black Teachers in the Urban South, 1865–1890," *Journal of Southern History* 40 (November 1974), 565–94; Edmund L. Drago, *Initiative, Paternalism, and Race Relations: Charleston's Avery Normal Institute* (Athens: University of Georgia Press, 1990), 174–76, 183.

17 W. T. B. Williams to Clarence Richmond, July 4, 1918, box 6, Williams Papers, Hollis B. Frissell Library, Tuskegee University.

18 Jones, *Negro Schools in the Southern States*, 69–70; Roscoe Conkling Bruce, "Tuskegee Institute," in *From Servitude to Service* (New York: Negro Universities Press, 1905, 1969), 113.

19 Powdermaker, *After Freedom*, 299.

20 W. E. B. Du Bois, "Outline of Report on the Economic Conditions of Negroes in the State of Texas," *Prairie View Standard* 27.2 (November 1935), 97–98. See also Horace Mann Bond, *The Education of the Negro in the American Social Order* (New York: Prentice-Hall, 1934), 12–13.

21 J. Morgan Kousser, "Progressivism—For Middle-Class Whites Only: North Carolina Education, 1880–1910," *Journal of Southern History* 46 (May 1980), 190. See also Bond, *Education of the Negro*, 169–71; Louis R. Harlan, *Separate and Unequal: Public School Campaigns and Racism in the Southern Seaboard States, 1901–1915* (Chapel Hill: University of North Carolina Press, 1958), 259–66.

22 Ronald E. Ferguson, "Shifting Challenges: Fifty Years of Economic Change Toward Black-White Earnings Equality," *Daedalus* 124 (winter 1995), 42–46; Samuel Bowles and Herbert Gintis, *Schooling in Capitalist America: Educational Reform and the Contradictions of Economic Life* (New York: BasicBooks, 1976), 35.

23 Walter Feinberg, *Reason and Rhetoric: The Intellectual Foundations of Twentieth-Century Liberal Educational Policy* (New York: John Wiley and Sons, 1975); Ira Katznelson and Margaret Weir, *Schooling for All: Class, Race, and the Decline of the Democratic Ideal* (New York: BasicBooks, 1985); Clarence J. Karier, "Testing for Order and Control in the Liberal State," in Clarence J. Karier, Paul C. Violas, and Joel Spring, eds., *Roots of Crisis: American Education in the Twentieth Century* (Chicago: Rand McNally, 1973), 108–37; Bowles and Gintis, *Schooling in Capitalist America*, 8. For a useful summary and critique of the work of these students of educational history, see Diane Ravitch, *The Revisionists Revised: A Critique of the Radical Attack on the Schools* (New York: BasicBooks, 1978).

24 Geo. F. Bowles to D. Burt, November 22, 1866, roll 47, Freedmen's Bureau Papers, Tennessee; Drago, *Initiative, Paternalism, and Race Relations*, 130–34; Lura Beam, *He Called Them by the Lightning: A Teacher's Odyssey in the Rural South, 1908–1919* (Indianapolis: Bobbs-Merrill, 1967), 3–4;

Willard B. Gatewood, *Aristocrats of Color: The Black Elite, 1880–1920* (Bloomington: Indiana University Press, 1990), 22–24, 83–85; Joel Williamson, *New People: Miscegenation and Mulattoes in the United States* (New York: Free Press, 1980), 127–33; Don H. Doyle, *New Men, New Cities, New South: Atlanta, Nashville, Charleston, Mobile, 1860–1910* (Chapel Hill: University of North Carolina Press, 1990), 273-78; Adam Fairclough, *Race and Democracy: The Civil Rights Struggle in Louisiana, 1915–72* (Athens: University of Georgia Press, 1995), 14–16.

25 C. J. C. Drake to D. Burt, December 6, 1866, roll 47, Freedmen's Bureau Papers, Tennessee; Richard R. Wright Jr., *Eighty-seven Years Behind the Black Curtain: An Autobiography* (Philadelphia: Rare Book Co., 1965), 31–32; Richard Brodhead, ed., *The Journals of Charles W. Chesnutt* (Durham: Duke University Press, 1993), 82.

26 Mansfield, "That Fateful Class," 251–56; Mildred D. G. Gallot, *A History of Grambling State University* (Lanham MD: University Press of America, 1985), 12–28; Booker T. Washington, "Extracts from an Address in Birmingham," January 1, 1900, in Louis R. Harlan et al., eds., *The Booker T. Washington Papers* (Urbana: University of Illinois Press, 1976), 5:284; "Extracts from an Address in Brooklyn," December 8, 1908, *ibid.* (1980), 9:417–20. For Washington's most controversial criticism of black ministers, see "A Speech Delivered Before the Women's New England Club, Boston," January 27, 1890, *ibid.* (1974), 3:27.

27 Donald Spivey, *Schooling for the New Slavery: Black Industrial Education, 1868–1915* (Westport CT: Greenwood Press, 1978); Elizabeth Jacoway, *Yankee Missionaries: The Penn School Experiment* (Baton Rouge: Louisiana State University Press, 1980); James D. Anderson, "Education as a Vehicle for the Manipulation of Black Workers," in Walter Feinberg and Henry Rosemont, eds., *Technology and Education: Dissenting Essays in the Intellectual Foundations of American Education* (Urbana: University of Illinois Press, 1975), 15–40; Bond, *Education of the Negro,* 404–10; Harlan, *Separate and Unequal* (Chapel Hill: University of North Carolina Press, 1958); Louis R. Harlan, *Booker T. Washington: The Making of a Black Leader, 1856–1901* (New York: Oxford University Press, 1972), 324; Louis R. Harlan, *Booker T. Washington: The Wizard of Tuskegee, 1901–1915* (New York: Oxford University Press, 1983); John H. Stanfield, *Philanthropy and Jim Crow in American Social Science* (Westport CT: Greenwood

Press, 1985); Karen J. Ferguson, "Caught in 'No Man's Land': The Negro Cooperative Demonstration Service and the Ideology of Booker T. Washington, 1900–1918," *Agricultural History* 72.1 (winter 1998), 33–54; Kousser, "Progressivism—For Middle-Class Whites Only," 169–94; Robert G. Newby and David B. Tyack, "Victims Without 'Crimes': Some Historical Perspectives on Black Education," *Journal of Negro Education* 40 (summer 1971), 192–206; Lester C. Lamon, "Black Public Education in the South, 1861–1920: By Whom, For Whom and Under Whose Control?" *Journal of Thought* 18.3 (fall 1983), 76–89.

28   Langston Hughes, "Cowards from the Colleges," *The Crisis* (August 1934), 226–28; Ralph Ellison, *Invisible Man* (New York: Vintage, 1952, 1972), 34–148; J. Saunders Redding, *Stranger and Alone* (New York: Harcourt, Brace, 1950); J. Saunders Redding, *On Being Negro in America* (New York: Bobbs-Merrill, 1951; reprint, New York: Bantam, 1964), 66–67; Lewis K. McMillan, "Negro Higher Education as I Have Known It," *Journal of Negro Education* 8 (January 1939), 14–15.

29   Michael Fultz, "African American Teachers in the South: Powerlessness and the Ironies of Expectations and Protest," *History of Education Quarterly* 35 (winter 1995), 416.

30   Drago, *Initiative, Paternalism, and Race Relations*, 177; Horace Mann Bond and Julia W. Bond, *The Star Creek Papers: Washington Parish and the Lynching of Jerome Wilson*, ed. Adam Fairclough (Athens: University of Georgia Press, 1997), 43–45; "Howard W. McElrath, an Interview," May 1940, box 2, Edward E. Strong Papers, Moorland-Spingarn Library, Howard University, Washington DC.

31   Alferdteen B. Harrison, *Piney Woods School: An Oral History* (Jackson: University of Mississippi Press, 1982), 109, 116; Arnold Cooper, *Between Struggle and Hope: Four Black Educators in the South, 1884–1915* (Ames: Iowa State University Press, 1989), 51–62; Prentiss Headlight, "The 'Little Professor' of Piney Woods Speaks," April 2, 1959, unidentified newspaper clipping in folder 9/19, Mississippi State Sovereignty Commission files, State Archives, Jackson.

32   Haley, *Charles–Hunter*, 285.

33   Glenda Elizabeth Gilmore, *Gender and Jim Crow: Women and the Politics of White Supremacy in North Carolina, 1896–1920* (Chapel Hill: University of North Carolina Press, 1996), 186. Gilmore used this term to describe

Charlotte Hawkins Brown, founder of Palmer Memorial Institute, a private girls school in Sedalia, North Carolina.

34 Washington, "A Speech Before the Philosophical Lyceum of Lincoln University," April 26, 1888, in Harlan, *The Booker T. Washington Papers,* 2:442; "An Abraham Lincoln Memorial Address in Philadelphia," February 14, 1899, *ibid.,* 5:32–38; "An Interview by Frank G. Carpenter in the *Memphis Commercial-Appeal,*" December 2, 1899, *ibid.,* 5:279–82; "An Address before the White Conference on the Care of Children," *ibid.,* 10:19–20; Washington to William P. Blake, December 12, 1911, *ibid.,* 11:413.

35 Elizabeth L. Wheeler, "Isaac Fisher: The Frustrations of a Negro Educator at Branch Normal College, 1902–1911," *Arkansas Historical Quarterly* 41 (spring 1982), 43; Emma L. Thornbrough, "Booker T. Washington as Seen by his White Contemporaries," *Journal of Negro History* 53 (April 1968), 179.

36 Stuart Grayson Noble, *Forty Years of the Public Schools in Mississippi: With Special Reference to the Education of the Negro* (New York: Negro Universities Press, 1918, 1969), 110–11; J. H. Phillips, "The Essential Requirements of Negro Education," in *Journal of Proceedings and Addresses, Nineteenth Annual Session, Atlanta, Georgia, December 29–31, 1908* (Atlanta: Southern Education Association, 1908), 123–26.

37 Washington, "A Speech before the National Educational Association," July 16, 1884, in Harlan, *The Booker T. Washington Papers,* 2:259; Virginia L. Denton, *Booker T. Washington and the Adult Education Movement* (Gainesville: University Press of Florida, 1993), 139–42; Richard D. Ralston, "American Episodes in the Making of an African Leader: A Case Study of Alfred B. Xuma," *International Journal of African Historical Studies* 6 (1973), 76.

38 Booker T. Washington, *Up From Slavery* (New York: Norton, 1901, 1996), 23–24; Charles S. Johnson, "Democracy and Social Control in Race Relations" (1942), box 160, folder 15, Charles S. Johnson Papers.

TWO *Robert R. Moton and the Travail of the Black College President*

1 Anderson, *Education of Blacks,* 36–46; Robert Francis Engs, *Educating the Disfranchised and Disinherited: Samuel Chapman Armstrong and*

Hampton Institute, 1839–1893 (Knoxville: University of Tennessee Press, 1999).

2 Robert R. Moton, "Inaugural Address," May 25, 1916, box 9, folder 61, Robert Russa Moton Papers, Hollis Burke Frissell Library, Tuskegee University.

3 *New York World*, May 30, 1916; Moton to S. L. Smith, September 5, 1916, box 6, folder 30; Moton to Fred R. Moore, June 3, 1916, box 10, folder 70, Moton Papers.

4 John A. Chambliss to Moton, June 15, 1916, box 11, folder 81; Seth Low to Moton, June 3, 1916, box 10, folder 66, Moton Papers.

5 Louis R. Harlan, *Booker T. Washington: The Making of a Black Leader, 1856–1901* (New York: Oxford University Press, 1972), 324; John M. Barry, *Rising Tide: The Great Mississippi Flood of 1927 and How It Changed America* (New York: Simon and Schuster, 1997), 322.

6 James Weldon Johnson, *Along This Way: The Autobiography of James Weldon Johnson* (New York: 1933, 1990), 313; Thomas Jesse Jones, *Negro Education: A Study of the Private and Higher Schools for Colored People in the United States* (Washington: Government Printing Office, 1917), 1:10–12, 55–60, 82–99; Kenneth J. King, *Pan-Africanism and Education: A Study of Race Philanthropy and Education in the Southern States of America and East Africa* (Oxford: Oxford University Press, 1971), 22–42.

7 Mark Ellis, "'Closing Ranks' and 'Seeking Honors': W. E. B. Du Bois in World War I," *Journal of American History* 79 (June 1992), 96–124.

8 "Robert Moton in France," *The Crisis* 18.1 (May 1919); Moton, report to the War Department, 1919; "General Summary," box 35, folder 234, Moton Papers. For the text of Moton's speech to black troops in France and a defense of his mission, see Albon L. Holsey, "A Man of Courage," in William Hardin Hughes and Frederick D. Patterson, eds., *Robert Russa Moton of Hampton and Tuskegee* (Chapel Hill: University of North Carolina Press, 1956), 123–27.

9 Leila B. Michael to Moton, May 5, 1919; letter to Moton (name of author illegible), March 24, 1919 (first quotation), box 58, folder 417, Moton Papers; Leroy Davis, *A Clashing of the Soul: John Hope and the Dilemma of African American Leadership and Black Higher Education in the Early Twentieth Century* (Athens: University of Georgia Press, 1998), 273 (second quotation). Moton defended his conduct in France in a private letter to

Du Bois, July 5, 1919; and in a public speech, July 24, 1919, both in folder 417, box 58, Moton Papers.

10 Raymond Wolters, *The New Negro on Campus: Black Campus Rebellions of the 1920s* (Princeton: Princeton University Press, 1975); McMillan, "Negro Higher Education," 14–15; Redding, *On Being Negro in America*, 66–67.

11 Lester C. Lamon, *Black Tennesseans, 1900–1930* (Knoxville: University of Tennessee Press, 1977), 103; Gerald L. Smith, *A Black Educator in the Segregated South: Kentucky's Rufus B. Atwood* (Lexington: University Press of Kentucky, 1994), 100–112; Joe M. Richardson, *A History of Fisk University, 1865–1946* (University: University of Alabama Press, 1980), 24–39; Robert R. Moton to George Foster Peabody, October 10, 1918, box 24, folder 163, Moton Papers; Isaac Fisher to Booker T. Washington, October 23, 1899, in Harlan, *The Booker T. Washington Papers*, 5:242; Wolters, *New Negro on Campus*, 230–75.

12 Ralph Ellison, *Invisible Man* (New York: Vintage, 1952, 1972), 140–41.

13 Langston Hughes, "Cowards from the Colleges," *Crisis*, 1934, 226–28.

14 Horace Mann Bond to Ralph Ellison, June 29, 1967, Horace Mann Bond Papers (microfilm), Perkins Library, Duke University. Bond was enraged that David Riesman and Cristopher Jencks, in their article "The American Negro College" (*Harvard Educational Review* 37.1 [1967]), wrote that Ellison's satirical portrait of a black college resembled reality. See Bond's unpublished article, "Jencks and Riesman—If My Students, I'd Flunk 'em Both!" also in the Bond Papers. See also Bond, "In Defense of Dr. Moton," *Chicago Defender*, September 7, 1929.

15 Martia G. Goodson, ed., *Chronicles of Faith: The Autobiography of Frederick D. Patterson* (Tuscaloosa: University of Alabama Press, 1991), 34.

16 Hughes and Patterson, *Robert Russa Moton*, 3–8.

17 Ibid., 9, 209.

18 National Education Association, *Proceedings of the Sixty-seventh Annual Meeting, Atlanta, June 28–July 4, 1929* (Washington DC: National Education Association, 1929), 107–11.

19 J. M. Springer to Moton, June 22, 1916; Moton to Springer, June 30, 1916, box 6, folder 31; W. B. Timberlake to Dear Sirs, April 10, 1916, box 6, folder 33, Moton Papers.

20 Moton to Woodrow Wilson, June 15, 25, 1918; box 26, folder 188; Moton

to George Foster Peabody, June 15, 29, 1918, box 24, folder 163, Moton Papers.

21 James H. Dillard to Moton, January 5, 1922, box 77, folder 537, Moton Papers.

22 Moton to Dillard, January 16, 1922, box 77, folder 537, Moton Papers.

23 Anson Phelps Stokes to Moton, December 8, 1916; Emmett J. Scott to Stokes, December 12, 1916, box 11, folder 89; Stokes to Scott, January 2, 1917, box 25, folder 176; Moton to Will A. Alexander, March 12, 1921, box 72, folder 478, Moton Papers.

24 Moton, "Address at the Dedication of the Lincoln Memorial," original text of speech, in Moton to William Howard Taft, May 17, 1922; "Address at the Dedication of the Lincoln Memorial," speech as delivered (revised with suggestions from the Lincoln Memorial Commission), May 30, 1922, box 11, folder 13, Robert R. Moton Papers, Library of Congress; *New York Times*, May 31, 1922.

25 Holsey, "A Man of Courage," 127–42; Robert J. Norrell, *Reaping the Whirlwind: The Civil Rights Movement in Tuskegee* (New York: Vintage, 1984), 27–30; Albon Holsey to James Weldon Johnson, April 2, 1923, box 90, folder 668; B. L. Bogeman to Moton, July 21, 1923, box 90, folder 669, Moton Papers; Walter White, *A Man Called White: The Autobiography of Walter White* (London: Victor Gollancz, 1949), 70.

26 Pete Daniel, "Black Power in the 1920s: The Case of the Tuskegee Veterans Hospital," *Journal of Southern History* 36 (August 1970), 363–88; Desmond King, "A Strong or a Weak State? Race and the U.S. Federal Government in the 1920s," *Ethnic and Racial Studies* 21 (January 1998), 21–47.

27 Barry, *Rising Tide*, 322–23, 381–95; Colored Advisory Committee, Preliminary Report, June 13, 1927; Moton to Herbert Hoover, October 1, 1927; Moton to J. S. Clark, December 16, 1927, box 135, folder 1; Moton, "Statement on Haiti," October 1, 1930, box 164, folder 1345; *Report of the U.S. Commission on Education in Haiti*, box 163, 1236; Moton to Hoover, January 15, March 9, March 31, 1931; Albon Holsey to Moton, February 26, 1931, Moton Papers.

28 Moton to Hoover, September 18, 1931; October 27, 1931; January 12, 1933; F. H. Payne, "Memorandum for the President," October 6, 1931, box 163, folder 1328, Moton Papers.

29 Frederick D. Patterson, "Administrator and Man," in Hughes and Pat-

terson, *Robert Russa Moton*, 224–25; Moton to James H. Dillard, January 16, 1922, box 77, folder 537; Moton to Melvin Chisum, December 10, 1932, box 170, folder 1417, Moton Papers.

30 Patterson, "Administrator and Man," 210–11; Moton to Trevor Arnett, March 9, 1929, box 170, folder 1423, Moton Papers; Robert R. Moton, *What the Negro Thinks* (Garden City NY: Doubleday, 1929).

31 Robert R. Moton to W. T. B. Williams, May 27, 1919, box 5, W. T. B. Williams Papers; W. T. B. Williams, "Is Tuskegee Just Another College?" *Journal of Educational Sociology* 7.3 (1933), 173–74; Jones, *Negro Schools in the South*, 60–63; Barry, *Rising Tide*, 379.

32 George R. Woolfolk, *Prairie View: A Study in Public Conscience, 1878–1946* (New York: Pageant Press, 1962), 108–98; Gilbert L. Porter and Leedell W. Neyland, *History of the Florida State Teachers Association* (Washington DC: National Education Association, 1977), 43–46; Raymond Wolters, *New Negro on Campus*, 194–97; Elizabeth Ross Haynes, *Unsung Heroes: The Black Boy of Atlanta* (New York: G. K. Hall, 1952, 1997), xxxi, 475.

33 John J. Coss, "Some Notes on Education in Southeast Georgia, June 15–19, 1936, with John Curtis Nixon," reel 333, Rosenwald Fund Papers (microfilm), Amistad Research Center, Tulane University; Range, *Rise and Progress of Negro Colleges*, 188.

34 W. T. B. Williams to W. R. Farrand, January 3, 1912, box 5, W. T. B. Williams Papers; Range, *Rise and Progress of Negro Colleges*, 185–88; Roger M. Williams, *The Bonds: An American Family* (New York: Athenaeum, 1972), 133, 139–40; Tom Dent, *Southern Journey: A Return to the Civil Rights Movement* (New York: William Morrow, 1997), 228–29.

35 Kenneth R. Warlick, "Practical Education and the Negro College in North Carolina, 1880–1930," Ph.D. diss., University of North Carolina, 1980, 401–9.

46 Anderson, *Education of Blacks*, 108–9, 273–75; [Sam Houston College], *The Bulletin*, January 19, 1908; *The Weekly Bulletin*, July 18, 1913; Jackson Davis, "Sam Houston College," November 2, 1916, reel 132, General Education Board Early Southern Programs: Texas (microfilm), Perry-Castañeda Library, University of Texas, Austin; Range, *Rise and Progress of Negro Colleges*, 185–88. Albany Institute eventually became a unit of the University of Georgia system.

37 Doug McAdam, *Political Process and the Development of Black Insurgency*,

1930–1970 (Chicago: University of Chicago Press, 1982), 93, 102; Goodson, *Chronicles of Faith*, 94–95.

38 Wendell Grant Morgan, "A Survey of the Social Science Offerings in Negro Colleges, 1935–1936," *Quarterly Review of Higher Education Among Negroes* 2 (1936), 169–79; Johnetta Richards, "The Southern Negro Youth Congress: A History," Ph.D. diss., University of Cincinnati, 1987, 17–32, 40–41, 49–56, 95–107, 137–47.

39 Urissa Rhone Brown, "My Leading Idea for the Week," July 31, 1950; "School Administration and Supervision in a Democracy," term paper, summer session, Prairie View College, 1950, both in Rhone Family Papers, collection 3U173, Barker Center for Texas History, University of Texas, Austin.

40 *Quarterly Review of Higher Education for Negroes* 1.1 (1933), 35; 2.1 (1934), 54; William I. Graham, "The Relation of Paine College to its Community," *Quarterly Review of Higher Education for Negroes* 4.3 (1936), 130; John A. Hardin, *Fifty Years of Segregation: Black Higher Education in Kentucky, 1904–1954* (Lexington: University Press of Kentucky, 1997), 52; Neil R. McMillen, *Dark Journey: Black Mississippians in the Age of Jim Crow* (Urbana: University of Illinois Press, 1990), 100; Leedell W. Neyland and John W. Riley, *The History of Florida Agricultural and Mechanical University* (Gainesville: University of Florida Press, 1963), 142.

41 Goodson, *Chronicles of Faith*, 34–35, 104–6.

42 Goodson, *Chronicles of Faith*, 58–61; Ralph David Abernathy, *And the Walls Came Tumbling Down* (New York: Harper and Row, 1989), 64–67.

43 Wilma Dykeman and James Stokely, *Seeds of Southern Change: The Life of Will Alexander* (New York: Norton, 1962, 1976), 67–72; Johnetta Richards, "The Southern Negro Youth Congress: A History," 40–56; Deborah Gray White, *Too Heavy a Load: Black Women in Defense of Themselves, 1894–1994* (New York: Norton, 1999), 148–50; Patricia Sullivan, *Days of Hope: Race and Democracy in the New Deal Era* (Chapel Hill: University of North Carolina Press, 1996), 99; John Egerton, *Speak Now Against the Day: The Generation Before the Civil Rights Movement in the South* (New York: Alfred A. Knopf, 1994), 284–87, 303–12.

44 Cecil J. Williams, *Freedom and Justice: Four Decades of the Civil Rights Struggle as Seen by a Black Photographer of the Deep South* (Macon: Mercer University Press, 1995), 97–122; Cristopher Jencks and David Riesman, *The Academic Revolution* (Garden City NY: Doubleday, 1968), 434; Smith,

A Black Educator, 155–62; Thelma D. Perry, *History of the American Teachers Association* (Washington DC: National Education Association, 1975), 315–18; Fairclough, *Race and Democracy*, 266–69.

45 K. H. Steele to Trenholm, March 11, 1960, box 26; excerpt from minutes of the meeting of the State Board of Education, March 23, 1960, box 30, Trenholm Papers.

46 Bennie D. Brown to H. Councill Trenholm, March 3, 1960; Alfred L. Brown to Trenholm, March 4, 1960; B. Hudson to Trenholm, n.d.; T. J. Austin to Trenholm, March 3, 1960, box 26, Trenholm Papers.

47 Lewis W. Jones, *Cold Rebellion: The South's Oligarchy in Revolt* (London: MacGibbon & Kee, 1962), 158; John W. Davis, "Tribute to H. Councill Trenholm," March 16, 1961, box 24, John W. Davis Papers, Moorland-Spingarn Library, Howard University; Jo Ann Gibson Robinson, *The Montgomery Bus Boycott and the Women Who Started It* (Knoxville: University of Tennessee Press, 1987), 50–52; *Mobile Register*, June 15, 1960; Floyd H. Mann to Trenholm, June 9, 1961, Classified Information File, box 26, Trenholm Papers; Andrew M. Manis, *A Fire You Can't Put Out: The Civil Rights Life of Birmingham's Fred L. Shuttlesworth* (Tuscaloosa: University of Alabama Press, 1999), 231–40.

48 Woolfolk, *Prairie View*, 330; Robert G. Sherer, *Subordination or Liberation: The Development of Conflicting Theories of Education in Nineteenth-Century Alabama* (University: University of Alabama Press, 1977), 26–28; "Annual Memorial-Tribute," December 14, 1959, box 26, Trenholm Papers; Transcript of Meeting of the Sub-Committee of Governor's Committee on Higher Education for Negroes in Alabama, March 26, 1949, Trenholm Papers.

49 Jacob L. Reddix, *A Voice Crying in the Wilderness: The Memoirs of Jacob L. Reddix* (Jackson: University Press of Mississippi, 1974), 222; Horace Mann Bond, "The Present Status of Racial Integration in the United States with Special Reference to Education," *Journal of Negro History* 21 (summer 1952), 250.

THREE *Black Teachers and the Civil Rights Movement*

1 Rosa Parks with Jim Haskins, *Rosa Parks: My Story* (New York: Scholastic, 1992), 49; Jones, *Negro Education*, 1:77–78.

2 Lewis W. Jones, "Fred L. Shuttlesworth: Indigenous Leader," in David J.

Garrow, ed., *Birmingham, Alabama, 1956–1963: The Black Struggle for Civil Rights* (Brooklyn: Carlson Publishing, 1989); Manis, *A Fire You Can't Put Out*, 29–30.

3 Andrew Young, *An Easy Burden: The Civil Rights Movement and the Transformation of America* (New York: HarperCollins, 1996), 18–19; biography of Williams in box 1, folder 2, Fannie C. Williams Papers, Amistad Research Center, Tulane University.

4 "A Tentative Approach to Negro History for Use in Grades 1–4 in New Orleans Colored Public Schools," box 2, folder 7; "Negro History Week," n.d., box 1, folder 7, George S. Longe Papers, Amistad Research Center, Tulane University; George Longe, "The Study of the Negro," *Crisis* 43 (October 1936), 304, 309; A. H. Parker, "Negro Pupils Plan Programs," *Nation's Schools* 23.4 (April 1939), 45; Jacqueline Goggin, *Carter G. Woodson: A Life in Black History* (Baton Rouge: Louisiana State University Press, 1993), 84, 119–20. On Carter G. Woodson and the Negro History movement, see also August Meier and Elliott Rudwick, *Black History and the Historical Profession, 1915–1980* (Urbana: University of Illinois Press, 1986), 7–62; Lorenzo J. Greene, *Selling Black History for Carter G. Woodson: A Diary, 1930–1933*, ed. Arvah E. Strickland (Columbia: University of Missouri Press, 1996).

5 Angela Davis, *Angela Davis: An Autobiography* (New York: International Publishers, 1974, 1988), 90–91.

6 Davis, *Autobiography*, 92–93; Young, *An Easy Burden*, 30–33; Dent, *Southern Journey*, 12–13, 329–31.

7 Miriam Feingold to Folks, August 19, 1963, reel 2, Feingold Papers (microfilm), State Historical Society of Wisconsin, Madison. See also, for example, Ronnie Moore, Louisiana Field Report, January–June, 1965, box 4, folder 1; Matthew Battiste, Scouting Report, April 14, 1964, box 6, folder 1, both in CORE Papers (Southern Regional Office), Madison State Historical Society. Similar criticisms of teachers are scattered throughout the papers of SNCC and SCLC.

8 Idus A. Newby, *Black Carolinians: A History of Blacks in South Carolina from 1865 to 1968* (Columbia: University of South Carolina Press, 1973), 82–94, 102–11, 258–73; Glenn T. Eskew, *But for Birmingham: The Local and National Movements in the Civil Rights Struggle* (Chapel Hill: University of North Carolina Press, 1997). Johnson was the father-in-law of General Colin Powell.

9 Bullock, *History of Negro Education in the South*, vii–ix; Leloudis, *Schooling the New South*, 223; Gunnar Myrdal, *An American Dilemma: The Negro Problem and Modern Democracy* (New York: Harper and Brothers, 1944), 2 : 881. For similarly positive assessments of black education, see for example Vaughan, *Schools for All*; Morris, *Reading, 'Riting, and Reconstruction*; Jones, *Soldiers of Light and Love*; Richardson, *Christian Reconstruction*; Heintze, *Private Black Colleges in Texas*, 11–13, 170; McPherson, *The Abolitionist Legacy*, 393.

10 Aldon D. Morris, *The Origins of the Civil Rights Movement: Black Communities Organizing for Change* (New York: Free Press, 1983); McAdam, *Political Process and the Development of Black Insurgency*; Norrell, *Reaping the Whirlwind*; William H. Chafe, *Civilities and Civil Rights: Greensboro, North Carolina, and the Black Struggle for Freedom* (New York: Oxford University Press, 1981). Sociologists Aldon Morris and Doug McAdam point to the importance of black colleges, along with churches and the NAACP, in producing the black insurgency. Historian Robert J. Norrell illustrates the crucial importance of Tuskegee Institute in shaping the Civil Rights movement in Tuskegee, Alabama. And in his study of Greensboro, North Carolina, William Chafe explores the role of schools and colleges in nurturing a democratic spirit that influenced the generation of 1960.

11 John Dittmer, *Local People: The Struggle for Civil Rights in Mississippi* (Urbana: University of Illinois Press, 1994), 75.

12 Bond, *Education of the Negro*, 274; Clark Foreman, *Environmental Factors in Negro Elementary Education* (New York: W. W. Norton, 1932), 40; State Department of Education, Alabama, "Report of a Survey of Wilcox County Schools, 1929–1930," box 1, series 12-6-14, Division of Negro Education, Georgia State Archives (collection hereinafter cited as DNE, Ga.); Fred McCuistion, *The South's Negro Teaching Force: A Study* (Nashville: Julius Rosenwald Fund, 1931), 6–8, 23–24.

13 John Simon, "Program in Rural Education" [1935], box 12-6-62, Division of Negro Education, Georgia State Archives; Foreman, *Environmental Factors in Negro Elementary Education*, 40; Arthur F. Raper, *Preface to Peasantry: A Tale of Two Black Belt Counties* (New York: Atheneum, 1936, 1968), 334; Myrdal, *An American Dilemma*, 2 : 902–3.

14 Charles S. Johnson, "The Cultural Environment of the Negro Child and its Educational Implications," February 15, 1939, box 160, folder 5, Charles S. Johnson Papers; Johnson, *Growing Up in the Black Belt*, 128–

34; Johnson, *The Negro Public Schools*, 107. See also Allison Davis and John Dollard, *Children of Bondage: The Personality Development of Negro Youth* (Washington DC: American Council on Education, 1940), 280–86.

15 Robinson, *The Bell Rings at Four*, 33, 39–42, 45.

16 "The Mineral Springs School"; "Mrs. E. M. Riddle's Report" [1934], box 335, folder 1, Julius Rosenwald Fund Papers, Fisk University; biographical information on Riddle from Darlene Clark Hine, "Mabel K. Staupers and the Integration of Black Nurses into the Armed Forces," in John Hope Franklin and August Meier, eds., *Black Leaders of the Twentieth Century* (Urbana: University of Illinois Press, 1982), 243. The school was located in Mineral Springs, an all-black community near Calhoun, in Ouchita Parish, Louisiana.

17 W. T. B. Williams to T. E. Rivers, July 8, 1920, box 6, Williams Papers; *Report of the Committee of Investigation of Certain Phases of Negro Education in Louisiana* [1930], box 4, folder 4, Longe Papers; McCuistion, *The South's Negro Teaching Force*, 8–9, 18–21, 25; Truman M. Pierce et al., *White and Negro Schools in the South: An Analysis of Biracial Education* (Englewood Cliffs NJ: Prentice-Hall, 1955), 192–201. In 1929 nearly half of Louisiana's black teachers attended summer schools of between six and twelve weeks.

18 Anderson, *Education of Blacks*, 197–223; Bond, *Education of the Negro*, 404–10; Lance G. E. Jones, *The Jeanes Teacher in the United States, 1908–1933* (Chapel Hill: University of North Carolina Press, 1937), 111; Abraham Flexner to Julius Rosenwald, January 30, 1925, Conference on High Schools for Negroes, General Education Board, New York, April 30, 1925, box 129, folder 8; Executive Committee Minutes, August 14, 1928, box 77, folder 5, Julius Rosenwald Fund Papers, Fisk University (collection hereinafter cited as JRF); Ira D. Bryant, *The Development of the Houston Negro Public Schools* (Houston: Phillis Wheatley High School, 1935), 17–18; *Booker T. Washington High School, Eagle, 1928*, box 3, folder 5, Rev. Jack Yates Family and Antioch Baptist Church Collection, Houston Metropolitan Research Center. Texas was, to be sure, ahead of most other southern states in the matter of black high schools. In 1915 it had more public high schools for blacks than any other southern state, and as late as 1940 boasted the largest percentage of blacks enrolled in secondary education in the South, excluding Missouri and West Virginia.

19   Thomas Jesse Jones to Rossa B. Cooley, March 13, 1929, box 133, folder 1014a, Moton Papers; John Simon, "Negro Trade Schools and States Colleges," 1936, box 127, folder 11, Rosenwald Fund Papers.

20   Johnson, *Growing Up in The Black Belt*, 194–98; Johnson, *The Negro Public Schools*, 152–59; R. Clyde Minor to Nathan C. Newbold, April 10, 1934, box 1, Special Subject File, DNI, NC; Simon, "Negro Trade Schools and State Colleges;" "Visit to Prairie View State College," February 17, 1940, roll 132, General Education Board Papers, Early Southern Programs, Texas.

21   Johnson, *The Negro Public Schools*, 52, 85–86; Straight University, Commencement, 1892, box 4, folder 1, Longe Papers; Reddix, *A Voice Crying in the Wilderness*, 139.

22   Leloudis, *Schooling the New South*, xiii, 187. According to Leloudis, 86 percent of North Carolina's white teachers were women by 1920.

23   Hortense Powdermaker, *Stranger and Friend: The Way of an Anthropologist* (New York: Norton, 1966), 144, 148–49; Gilmore, *Gender and Jim Crow*, 148.

24   Powdermaker, *After Freedom*, 367; Ambrose Caliver, *A Background Study of Negro College Students* (Westport CT: Negro Universities Press, 1933, 1970), 43–44.

25   Caliver, *Background Study*, 26; Johnson, *The Negro Public Schools*, 18; Ambrose Caliver, *A Personnel Study of Negro College Students* (Westport CT: Negro Universities Press, 1931, 1970), 116–18.

26   Stephanie J. Shaw, *What a Woman Ought to Be and to Do: Black Professional Women Workers During the Jim Crow Era* (Chicago: University of Chicago Press, 1996), 219.

27   Booker T. Washington, "Extracts from an Address at Carnegie Hall," February 23, 1909, in Harlan, *Washington Papers*, 10 : 51; Estelle Massey Riddle, "The Mineral Springs School"; "The Mineral Springs Community" [1934], box 335, folder 1, Rosenwald Fund Papers.

28   Leon Litwack, *Trouble in Mind: Black Southerners in the Age of Jim Crow* (New York: Alfred A. Knopf, 1998), 83–85; Jones, *Cold Rebellion*, 128; Marshall Fred Phillips, "A History of the Public Schools in Birmingham, Alabama," M.A. thesis, University of Alabama, 1939, 111–13; *"A Dream Come True": Autobiography of Arthur Harold Parker* (Birmingham AL: Birmingham Industrial High School, 1932–33), 57–58.

29 In 1904 black teachers formed the National Association of Negro Teachers (renamed the National Association of Teachers in Colored Schools, 1907; the American Teachers Association, 1937). A parallel association of black PTAS appeared shortly thereafter. The presidents of black state colleges began meeting in 1901; in 1923 they strengthened their collaboration by forming the Association of Negro Land-grant Colleges. Seven years later an Association of Colleges for Negro Youth made its debut (renamed the Association of Colleges and Secondary Schools in 1934). In 1947 NCOSTA, the National Conference of State Teachers Associations, was organized. See Perry, *History of the American Teachers Association*, 42; Woolfolk, *Prairie View*, 236–37; Leland Stanford Cozart, *A History of the Association of Colleges and Secondary Schools* (Charlotte NC: Association of Colleges and Secondary Schools, 1965), 2–7; Melanie Carter, "From Jim Crow to Inclusion: An Historical Analysis of the Association of Colleges and Secondary Schools for Negroes," Ph.D. diss., Ohio State University, 1996.

30 *The Moving Finger* 5 (1939), magazine of Valena C. Jones Normal School, box 2, folder 5, Fannie C. Williams Papers. Williams served as president of the American Teachers Association in 1930.

31 "Negro Education, Third Progress Report," Education 271—Curriculum Studies, Louisiana State University, summer 1937, roll 69, General Education Board, Early Southern Programs, Louisiana; "The Open Road: A Teacher's Guide to Child and Community Development," 1937, box 2, series 12-6-71, Division of Negro Education, Georgia; "Program for Public Education in Tennessee," 1936, roll 411, RG 92, Department of Education, Tennessee.

32 John C. Dixon to William Crowe, August 16, 1939, box 103, folder 16, Rosenwald Fund Papers; Commission on Secondary Schools of the Association of Colleges and Secondary Schools for Negroes, *Progress and Plans of Negro High Schools Toward Regional Accreditation, 1944–45*, roll 411, RG 92, Division of Education, Tennessee.

33 For an overview of the salaries equalization campaign, see Mark V. Tushnet, *The NAACP's Legal Strategy Against Segregated Education, 1925–1950* (Chapel Hill: University of North Carolina Press, 1987), 58–65, 77–81, 88–104.

34 J. C. Dixon to Superintendents, September 20, 1932; Guy Wells to

Dixon, October 19, 1932; Walter T. J. Dempsey Jr. to Dixon, November 10, 1932, box 1, series 12-6-62; Grant to Cousins, March 11, 1941; Cousins to M. D. Collins et al., March 13, 1941; "Meeting of Joint Committee of State Teachers Association and Georgia Association of Colleges and Secondary Schools," March 10, 1941, Robert L. Cousins to James L. Grant, February 26, 1941, box 3, series 12-6-71, Division of Negro Education, Georgia; "Walter Chivers Says—Attention, Again, Georgia Teachers," *Atlanta Daily World*, March 12, 1941; Walter White to Eugene Martin, December 9, 1941; Martin to White, December 13, December 29, 1941, part 3, series B, NAACP papers (microfilm); Donald L. Grant, *The Way it Was in the South: The Black Experience in Georgia* (New York: Birch Lane Press, 1993), 356–57.

35 J. W. Nicolson to Thurgood Marshall, March 17, 1941; Memo to Mr. Marshall from Mr. Thomas, December 7, 1942; Mrs. B. D. McDaniel to Walter White, September 29, 1944; Leslie Perry to Walter White and Thurgood Marshall, "Visit to Mississippi State Teachers Conference," November 4, 1944, summary of salary equalization cases, January 18, 1947, part 3, series B, NAACP papers (microfilm); Rupert Picott, *History of the Virginia Teachers Association* (Washington DC: National Education Association, 1975), 110–20; Porter and Neyland, *History of the Florida State Teachers Association*, 64–65; Fairclough, *Race and Democracy*, 62–63, 71; Raymond Gavins, "The NAACP in North Carolina During the Age of Segregation," in Armstead L. Robinson and Patricia L. Sullivan, eds., *New Directions in Civil Rights Studies* (Charlottesville: University Press of Virginia, 1991), 105–25; Perry, *History of the American Teachers Association*, 263–64; Shaw, *What a Woman Ought to Be and to Do*, 203. In North Carolina and West Virginia equalization was achieved without recourse to litigation.

36 Harry S. Ashmore, *The Negro and the Schools* (Chapel Hill: University of North Carolina Press, 1954); Numan V. Bartley, *The New South, 1945–1980* (Baton Rouge: Louisiana State University Press, 1995), 148–51; Augustus M. Burns III, "Graduate Education for Blacks in North Carolina, 1930–1951," *Journal of Southern History* 46 (May 1980), 195–218; Michael L. Gillette, "Heman L. Sweatt: Civil Rights Plaintiff," in Alwyn Barr and Robert A. Calvert, ed., *Black Leaders: Texans for Their Times* (Austin: Texas State Historical Association, 1981), 170; Neyland and

Riley, *History of Florida Agricultural and Mechanical University,* 250–64; Fairclough, *Race and Democracy,* 109.

37 Transcript of Meeting of the Sub-Committee of Governor's Committee on Higher Education for Negroes in Alabama, March 12, 1949, Trenholm Papers.

38 Cooke, *The White Superintendent and the Negro Schools in North Carolina,* 130; Minutes of Group Superintendents Meetings, Winston-Salem, May 28; Washington, May 31; Carthage, June 5, 1940, box 11, Special Subject Files, Division of Negro Education, Department of Public Instruction, North Carolina State Archives.

39 Anderson, *Education of Blacks,* 231–35; "Report to the Julius Rosenwald Fund on Survey in Birmingham, Alabama, to Determine Vocational Opportunities for Negro Youth," January 1930, box 546, folder 17; Charles S. Johnson, "Memorandum on the Displacement of Negro Workers in Certain Southern Cities," box 547, folder 4; Walter D. Cocking and Staff, "Outline for the Discussion of Higher Education for Negroes in Georgia," May 1938, box 546, folder 6; Bruce R. Payne to George R. James, August 30, 1938, box 128, folder 6, Rosenwald Fund Papers.

40 Fairclough, *Race and Democracy,* 84–98.

41 J. W. Seabrook to Newbold, April 22, 1934, box 1, both in Special Subject File, Department of Public Instruction, Division of Negro Education, North Carolina; Carleton Washburne, *A Summary Report of the Louisiana Educational Survey Commission* (Baton Rouge: Louisiana Educational Survey Commission, 1942), 105; Phillip S. Johnson, "Confronting the Dilemma: Charles S. Johnson's Study of Louisiana's Schools," *Louisiana History* 38 (spring 1997), 133–55; Joseph E. Gibson, "An Approach to the Problem of Vocational Education for Negroes," April 18, 1942, roll 67, General Education Board, Early Southern Programs, Louisiana.

42 Walter White to Anson Phelps Stokes, November 2, 1939, box 31, folder 11, Phelps-Stokes Fund Papers, Schomburg Library, New York City; "Discussion of Thurgood Marshall . . . at Meeting of Association of Colleges and Secondary Schools for Negroes," December 6, 1945, part 3, series B, NAACP Papers (microfilm).

43 W. E. B. Du Bois, *Dusk of Dawn: An Essay Toward an Autobiography of a Race Concept* (New York: Harcourt, Brace, 1940), 201; Du Bois, "A Philosophy of Race Segregation," *Quarterly Review of Higher Education for*

Negroes 3 (1936), 190–92; Constance Baker Motley, *Equal Justice Under Law: An Autobiography* (New York: Farrar, Straus and Giroux, 1998), 107; Jack Bass, "Interview with Constance Baker Motley," page 73, June 21, 1979, Jack Bass Oral History Collection, Law Library, Tulane University.

44 Nathan C. Newbold, "North Carolina Moves Positively Toward Equality in Public Education Between White and Colored People," January 4, 1950, box 1, Special Subject File, Division of Negro Education, North Carolina; Rufus B. Atwood, "The Public Negro College in a Racially Integrated System of Higher Education," *Journal of Negro Education* 21 (winter 1952), 352–63; NAACP Legal Defense and Educational Fund, "Program to Protect Teachers from Dismissal as a Result of Integration of Public Schools" [1955]; John W. Davis, "Memo to Mrs. Anna C. Frank: The Work of the Department of Teacher Information and Security, January 2–June 15, 1955," both in box 9, folder 13, John W. Davis Papers, Moorland-Spingarn Library, Howard University.

45 Thurgood Marshall, "Report on Department of Teacher Information and Security, January 1–June 30, 1955," box 9, folder 13; "Notes on Meeting of Georgia NAACP," June 16, 1955, box 33, folder 19, John W. Davis Papers; Williams, *Freedom and Justice*, 123–24.

46 "Notes on Meeting of Georgia NAACP," July 16, 1955, box 33, folder 19, John W. Davis Papers; Michael Shultz Jr., *The National Education Association and the Black Teacher: The Integration of a Professional Organization* (Coral Gables: University of Miami Press, 1970), 70–83; Walter White, "Some Tactics Which Should Supplement Resort to the Courts in Achieving Racial Integration in Education," *Journal of Negro Education* 21 (winter 1952), 340; "Negro Teachers and the Elimination of Segregated Schools," *Journal of Negro Education* 20 (spring 1951), 135–39; F. D. Patterson, "The Private Negro College in a Racially Integrated System of Higher Education," *Journal of Negro Education* 21 (winter 1952), 363–69; Motley, *Equal Justice Under Law*, 111.

47 Schultz, *National Education Association*, 150–201.

48 Bartley, *The New South*, 422–23; Dent, *Southern Journey*, 326.

49 Edmund Jefferson Oliver, *The End of an Era: Fairfield Industrial High School, 1924–1968* (Fairfield AL: privately published, 1968), copy in Birmingham Public Library.

50 Thomas Sowell, *Assumption Versus History: Collected Papers* (Stanford

CA: Hoover Institution Press, 1986), 7–37; Vanessa Siddle Walker, *Their Highest Potential: An African American School Community in the Segregated South* (Chapel Hill: University of North Carolina Press, 1996); David S. Cecelski, *Along Freedom Road: Hyde County, North Carolina, and the Fate of Black Schools in the South* (Chapel Hill: University of North Carolina Press, 1994), 173–74; Eldred Davis to Raymond Pitts, December 20, 1979, box 78, folder 21, American Missionary Association Papers, Amistad Research Center.

51 Oliver, *The End of an Era*, 44–45.

52 *Journal of Negro Education* 21 (winter 1952), 302.

53 Myrdal, *An American Dilemma*, 881; Gilmore, *Gender and Jim Crow*, 186; Zack J. Van Landigham, "NAACP, Taylorsville, Mississippi," November 14, 1958, series 3, file 80, State Sovereignty Commission Papers, Mississippi Department of Archives and History, Jackson.

54 Walker, *Their Highest Potential*, 219; Anderson, *Education of Blacks*, 285.

Bibliography

Abernathy, Ralph David. *And the Walls Came Tumbling Down: An Autobiography.* New York: Harper and Row, 1989.

Anderson, James D. "Education as a Vehicle for the Manipulation of Black Workers." In *Technology and Education: Dissenting Essays in the Intellectual Foundations of American Education.* Ed. Walter Feinberg and Henry Rosemount. Urbana: University of Illinois Press, 1975. 15–40.

———. *The Education of Blacks in the South, 1860–1935.* Chapel Hill: University of North Carolina Press, 1988.

———. "Ex-Slaves and the Rise of Universal Education in the New South, 1860–1880." In *Education and the Rise of the New South.* Ed. Ronald K. Goodenow and Arthur O. White. Boston: G. K. Hall, 1981. 1–25.

Ashmore, Harry S. *The Negro and the Schools.* Chapel Hill: University of North Carolina Press, 1954.

Atwood, Rufus B. "The Public Negro College in a Racially Integrated System of Higher Education." *Journal of Education* 21 (winter 1952): 352–63.

Barry, John M. *Rising Tide: The Great Mississippi Flood of 1927 and How It Changed America.* New York: Simon and Schuster, 1997.

Bartley, Numan V. *The New South, 1945–1980.* Baton Rouge: Louisiana State University Press, 1995.

Beam, Lura. *He Called Them by the Lightning: A Teacher's Odyssey in the Rural South, 1908–1919.* Indianapolis: Bobbs-Merrill, 1967.

Bond, Horace Mann. *The Education of the Negro in the American Social Order.* New York: Prentice-Hall, 1934.

———. "The Present Status of Racial Integration in the United States with Special Reference to Education." *Journal of Negro History* 21 (summer 1952): 241–50.

Bond, Horace Mann, and Julia W. Bond. *The Star Creek Papers: Washington Parish and the Lynching of Jerome Wilson.* Ed. Adam Fairclough. Athens: University of Georgia Press, 1997.

Bowles, Samuel, and Herbert Gintis. *Schooling in Capitalist America: Educa-*

tional *Reform and the Contradictions of Economic Life.* New York: Basic-Books, 1976.

Brodhead, Richard, ed. *The Journals of Charles W. Chesnutt.* Durham: Duke University Press, 1993.

Bruce, Roscoe Conkling. "Tuskegee Institute." In *From Servitude to Service: Being the Old South Lectures on the History and Work of Institutions for the Education of the Negro.* 1905. Reprint, with an introduction by Robert C. Ogden, New York: Negro Universities Press, 1969. 83–113.

Bryant, Ira D. *The Development of the Houston Negro Public Schools.* Houston: Phillis Wheatley High School, 1935.

Bullock, Henry Allen. *A History of Negro Education in the South: From 1619 to the Present.* Cambridge: Harvard University Press, 1967.

Burns, Augustus M., III. "Graduate Education for Blacks in North Carolina, 1930–1951." *Journal of Southern History* 46 (May 1980): 195–218.

Butchart, Ronald E. *Northern Schools, Southern Blacks, and Reconstruction, 1862–1875.* Westport CT: Greenwood Press, 1980.

Caliver, Ambrose. *A Personnel Study of Negro College Students.* 1931. Reprint, Westport CT: Negro Universities Press, 1970.

Carter, Melanie. "From Jim Crow to Inclusion: An Historical Analysis of the Association of Colleges and Secondary Schools for Negroes." Ph.D. diss., Ohio State University, 1996.

Cecelski, David S. *Along Freedom Road: Hyde County, North Carolina, and the Fate of Black Schools in the South.* Chapel Hill: University of North Carolina Press, 1994.

Chafe, William H. *Civilities and Civil Rights: Greensboro, North Carolina, and the Black Struggle for Freedom.* New York: Oxford University Press, 1981.

Cooper, Arnold. *Between Struggle and Hope: Four Black Educators in the South, 1869–1915.* Ames: Iowa State University Press, 1989.

Cozart, Leland Stanford. *A History of the Association of Colleges and Secondary Schools.* Charlotte: Association of Colleges and Secondary Schools, 1965.

Daniel, Pete. "Black Power in the 1920s: The Case of the Tuskegee Veterans Hospital." *Journal of Southern History* 36 (August 1970): 363–88.

Davis, Allison, and John Dollard. *Children of Bondage: The Personality Development of Negro Youth.* Washington DC: American Council of Education, 1940.

Davis, Angela. *Angela Davis: An Autobiography.* New York: International Publishers, 1988.

Davis, Leroy. *A Clashing of the Soul: John Hope and the Dilemma of African American Leadership and Black Higher Education in the Early Twentieth Century.* Athens: University of Georgia Press, 1998.

Dent, Tom. *Southern Journey: A Return to the Civil Rights Movement.* New York: William Morrow, 1997.

Denton, Virginia L. *Booker T. Washington and the Adult Education Movement.* Gainesville: University Press of Florida, 1993.

Dittmer, John. *Local People: The Struggle for Civil Rights in Mississippi.* Urbana: University of Illinois Press, 1994.

Doyle, Don H. *New Men, New Cities, New South: Atlanta, Nashville, Charleston, Mobile, 1860–1910.* Chapel Hill: University of North Carolina Press, 1990.

Drago, Edmund L. *Initiative, Paternalism, and Race Relations: Charleston's Avery Normal Institute.* Athens: University of Georgia Press, 1990.

Du Bois, W. E. B. *Dusk of Dawn: An Essay Toward an Autobiography of a Race Concept.* New York: Harcourt, Brace, 1940.

———. "A Philosophy of Race Segregation." *Quarterly Review of Higher Education for Negroes* 3 (1936): 189–94.

Du Bois, W. E. B., and August G. Dill. *The College-Bred Negro American.* Atlanta: Atlanta University Press, 1910; reprint, New York: Arno Press, 1968.

Dykeman, Wilma, and James Stokely. *Seeds of Southern Change: The Life of Will Alexander.* New York: Norton, 1976.

Egerton, John. *Speak Now Against the Day: The Generation Before the Civil Rights Movement in the South.* New York: Alfred A. Knopf, 1994.

Ellis, Mark. "'Closing Ranks' and 'Seeking Honors': W. E. B. Du Bois in World War I." *Journal of American History* 79 (June 1992): 96–124.

Ellison, Ralph. *Invisible Man.* 1952. Reprint, New York: Vintage, 1972.

Engs, Robert Francis. *Educating the Disfranchised and Disinherited: Samuel Chapman Armstrong and Hampton Institute, 1839–1893.* Knoxville: University of Tennessee Press, 1999.

Fairclough, Adam. *Race and Democracy: The Civil Rights Struggle in Louisiana, 1915–72.* Athens: University of Georgia Press, 1995.

Feinberg, Walter. *Reason and Rhetoric: The Intellectual Foundations of Twentieth-Century Liberal Educational Policy.* New York: John Wiley, 1975.

Ferguson, Karen J. "Caught in 'No Man's Land': The Negro Cooperative Demonstration Service and the Ideology of Booker T. Washington, 1900–1918." *Agricultural History* 72 (winter 1998): 33–54.

Ferguson, Ronald E. "Shifting Challenges: Fifty Years of Economic Change Toward Black-White Earnings Equality." *Daedalus* 124 (winter 1995): 37–76.

Foreman, Clark. *Environmental Factors in Negro Elementary Education.* New York: W. W. Norton, 1932.

Frazier, E. Franklin. *The Negro Family in the United States.* Chicago: University of Chicago Press, 1966.

Fultz, Michael. "African American Teachers in the South, 1890–1940: Powerlessness and the Ironies of Expectations and Protest." *History of Education Quarterly* 35 (winter 1995): 401–22.

Gallot, Mildred D. G. *A History of Grambling State University.* Lanham MD: University Press of America, 1985.

Gatewood, Willard B. *Aristocrats of Color: The Black Elite, 1880–1920.* Bloomington: Indiana University Press, 1990.

Gavins, Raymond. "The NAACP in North Carolina During the Age of Segregation." In *New Directions in Civil Rights Studies.* Ed. Armstead L. Robinson and Patricia L. Sullivan. Charlottesville: University Press of Virginia, 1991. 105–25.

Gilmore, Glenda Elizabeth. *Gender and Jim Crow: Women and the Politics of White Supremacy in North Carolina, 1896–1920.* Chapel Hill: University of North Carolina Press, 1996.

Goggin, Jacqueline. *Carter G. Woodson: A Life in Black History.* Baton Rouge: Louisiana State University Press, 1993.

Goodson, Martia G., ed. *Chronicles of Faith: The Autobiography of Frederick D. Patterson.* Tuscaloosa: University of Alabama Press, 1991.

Graham, William L. "The Relation of Paine College to its Community." *Quarterly Review of Higher Education for Negroes* 4 (1936): 129–33.

Grant, Donald L. *The Way It Was in the South: The Black Experience in Georgia.* New York: Birch Lane Press, 1993.

Greene, Lorenzo J. *Selling Black History for Carter G. Woodson: A Diary.* Ed. Arvah E. Strickland. Columbia: University of Missouri Press, 1996.

Haley, John H. *Charles N. Hunter and Race Relations in North Carolina.* Chapel Hill: University of North Carolina Press, 1987.

Hardin, John A. *Fifty Years of Segregation: Black Higher Education in Kentucky, 1904–1954.* Lexington: University Press of Kentucky, 1997.

Harlan, Louis R. *Booker T. Washington: The Making of a Black Leader, 1856–1901.* New York: Oxford University Press, 1972.

———. *Booker T. Washington: The Wizard of Tuskegee.* New York: Oxford University Press, 1983.

———. *Separate and Unequal: Public School Campaigns and Racism in the Southern Seaboard States, 1901–1915.* Chapel Hill: University of North Carolina Press, 1958.

Harlan, Louis R., et al., eds. *The Booker T. Washington Papers.* 14 vols. Urbana: University of Illinois Press, 1972–89.

Harrison, Alferdteen B. *Piney Woods School: An Oral History.* Jackson: University of Mississippi Press, 1982.

Haynes, Elizabeth Ross. *Unsung Heroes; The Black Boy of Atlanta; Negroes in Domestic Service in the United States.* New York: G. K. Hall, 1952, 1997.

Heintze, Michael R. *Private Black Colleges in Texas, 1865–1954.* College Station: Texas A&M University Press, 1985.

Hine, Darlene Clark. "Mabel K. Staupers and the Integration of Black Nurses into the Armed Forces." In *Black Leaders of the Twentieth Century.* Ed. John Hope Franklin and August Meier. Urbana: University of Illinois Press, 1982.

Hughes, Langston. "Cowards from the Colleges." *Crisis,* August 1934, 226–28.

Hughes, William Hardin, and Frederick D. Patterson, eds. *Robert Russa Moton of Hampton and Tuskegee.* Chapel Hill: University of North Carolina Press, 1956.

Jacoway, Elizabeth. *Yankee Missionaries: The Penn School Experiment.* Baton Rouge: Louisiana State University Press, 1980.

Jencks, Cristopher, and David Riesman. *The Academic Revolution.* Garden City NY: Doubleday, 1968.

Johnson, Charles S. *Growing up in the Black Belt: Negro Youth in the Rural South.* 1941. Reprint, New York: Schocken Books, 1967.

———. *The Negro Public Schools: A Social and Educational Survey.* Baton Rouge: Louisiana Educational Survey Commission, 1942.

Johnson, James Weldon. *Along This Way: The Autobiography of James Weldon Johnson.* 1933. Reprint, New York: Penguin, 1990.

Johnson, Phillip S. "Confronting the Dilemma: Charles S. Johnson's Study of Louisiana's Schools." *Louisiana History* 38 (spring 1997): 133–55.

Jones, Jacqueline. *Soldiers of Light and Love: Northern Teachers and Georgia Blacks, 1865–1875.* Athens: University of Georgia Press, 1992.

Jones, Lance G. E. *The Jeanes Teachers in the United States, 1908–1933.* Chapel Hill: University of North Carolina Press, 1937.

———. *Negro Schools in the Southern States.* Oxford: Clarendon Press, 1928.

Jones, Lewis W. *Cold Rebellion: The South's Oligarchy in Revolt.* London: MacGibbon and Kee, 1962.

———. "Fred L. Shuttlesworth: Indigenous Leader." In *Birmingham, Alabama, 1956–1963: The Black Struggle for Civil Rights.* Ed. David J. Garrow. Brooklyn: Carlson, 1989. 115–50.

Jones, Thomas Jesse. *Negro Education: A Study of the Private and Higher Schools for Colored People in the United States.* 2 vols. Washington DC: Government Printing Office, 1917.

Karier, Clarence J. "Testing for Order and Control in the Liberal State." In *Roots of Crisis: American Education in the Twentieth Century.* Ed. Paul C. Violas and Joel Spring. Chicago: Rand McNally, 1973. 108–37.

Katznelson, Ira, and Margaret Weir. *Schooling for All: Class, Race, and the Decline of the Democratic Ideal.* New York: BasicBooks, 1985.

King, Desmond. "A Strong or a Weak State? Race and the U.S. Federal Government in the 1920s." *Ethnic and Racial Studies* 21 (January 1998): 21–47.

King, Kenneth J. *Pan-Africanism and Education: A Study of Race Philanthropy in the Southern States of America and East Africa.* Oxford: Oxford University Press, 1971.

Kousser, J. Morgan. "Progressivism—For Middle-Class Whites Only: North Carolina Education, 1880–1910." *Journal of Southern History* 46 (May 1980): 169–94.

Lamon, Lester C. "Black Public Education in the South, 1861–1920: By Whom, For Whom, and Under Whose Control?" *Journal of Thought* 18 (fall 1983): 76–89.

———. *Black Tennesseans, 1900–1930.* Knoxville: University of Tennessee Press, 1977.

Leloudis, James L. *Schooling the New South: Pedagogy, Self, and Society in North Carolina, 1880–1920.* Chapel Hill: University of North Carolina Press, 1996.

Litwack, Leon. *Trouble in Mind: Black Southerners in the Age of Jim Crow.* New York: Alfred A. Knopf, 1998.

Longe, George. "The Study of the Negro." *Crisis* 43 (October 1936): 304, 309.

Manis, Andrew M. *A Fire You Can't Put Out: The Civil Rights Life of Birming-ham's Fred L. Shuttlesworth.* Tuscaloosa: University of Alabama Press, 1999.

Mansfield, Betty. "That Fateful Class: Black Teachers of Virginia's Freedmen, 1861–1882." Ph.D. diss., Catholic University of America, 1980.

McAdam, Doug. *Political Process and the Development of Black Insurgency, 1930–1970.* Chicago: University of Chicago Press, 1982.

McCuistion, Fred. *The South's Negro Teaching Force: A Study.* Nashville: Julius Rosenwald Fund, 1931.

McMillan, Lewis K. "Negro Higher Education as I Have Known It." *Journal of Negro Education* 8 (January 1939): 9–18.

McMillen, Neil R. *Dark Journey: Black Mississippians in the Age of Jim Crow.* Urbana: University of Illinois Press, 1990.

McPherson, James M. *The Abolitionist Legacy: From Reconstruction to the NAACP.* Princeton: Princeton University Press, 1975, 1995.

Meier, August, and Elliott Rudwick. *Black History and the Historical Profession, 1915–1980.* Urbana: University of Illinois Press, 1986.

Morris, Aldon D. *The Origins of the Civil Rights Movement: Black Communities Organizing for Change.* New York: Free Press, 1983.

Morris, Robert C. *Reading, 'Riting, and Reconstruction: The Education of Freed-men in the South, 1861–1870.* Chicago: University of Chicago Press, 1982.

Motley, Constance Baker. *Equal Justice Under Law: An Autobiography.* New York: Farrar, Straus and Giroux, 1998.

Moton, Robert R. *What the Negro Thinks.* Garden City NY: Doubleday, 1929.

Myrdal, Gunnar. *An American Dilemma: The Negro Problem and Modern De-mocracy.* 2 vols. New York: Harper and Brothers, 1944.

Newbold, Nathan C. *Five North Carolina Negro Educators.* Chapel Hill: University of North Carolina Press, 1939.

Newby, Robert G., and David B. Tyack. "Victims Without Crimes: Some Historical Perspectives on Black Education." *Journal of Negro Education* 40 (summer 1971): 192–206.

Neyland, Leedell W., and John W. Riley. *The History of Florida Agricultural and Mechanical University.* Gainesville: University of Florida Press, 1963.

Noble, Stuart Grayson. *Forty Years of the Public Schools in Mississippi: With Special Reference to the Education of the Negro.* 1918. Reprint, New York: Negro Universities Press, 1969.

Norrell, Robert J. *Reaping the Whirlwind: The Civil Rights Movement in Tuskegee.* New York: Vintage, 1984.

Oliver, Edmond Jefferson. *The End of an Era: Fairfield Industrial High School, 1924–1928.* Fairfield AL: [privately published], 1968.

Parker, A. H. *"A Dream Come True": Autobiography of Arthur Harold Parker.* Birmingham AL: Birmingham Industrial High School, 1932.

———. "Negro Pupils Plan Progress." *Nation's Schools* 23 (April 1939): 45.

Parks, Rosa, with Jim Haskins. *Rosa Parks: My Story.* New York: Scholastic, 1992.

Patterson, F. D. "The Private Negro College in a Racially Integrated System of Higher Education." *Journal of Negro Education* 21 (winter 1952): 363–69.

Perry, Thelma D. *History of the American Teachers Association.* Washington DC: National Education Association, 1975.

Phillips, Marshall Fred. "A History of the Public Schools in Birmingham, Alabama." M.A. thesis, University of Alabama, 1938.

Picott, Rupert J. *History of the Virginia Teachers Association.* Washington DC: National Education Association, 1975.

Pierce, Truman M., et al. *White and Negro Schools in the South: An Analysis of Biracial Education.* Englewood Cliffs NJ: Prentice-Hall, 1955.

Porter, Gilbert L., and Leedell W. Neyland. *History of the Florida State Teachers Association.* Washington DC: National Education Association, 1977.

Powdermaker, Hortense. *After Freedom: A Cultural Study in the Deep South.* 1939. Reprint, New York: Atheneum, 1969.

———. *Stranger and Friend: The Way of an Anthropologist.* New York: W. W. Norton, 1966.

Rabinowitz, Howard N. "Half a Loaf: The Shift from White to Black Teachers in the Urban South, 1865–1890." *Journal of Southern History* 40 (November 1974): 565–94.

Ralston, Richard D. "American Episodes in the Making of an African Leader: A Case Study of Alfred B. Xuma." *International Journal of African Historical Studies* 6 (1973): 72–93.

Range, Willard. *The Rise and Progress of Negro Colleges in Georgia, 1865–1949.* Athens: University of Georgia Press, 1951.

Raper, Arthur F. *Preface to Peasantry: A Tale of Two Black Belt Counties.* 1936. Reprint, New York: Atheneum, 1968.

Ravitch, Diane. *The Revisionists Revised: A Critique of the Radical Attack on the Schools.* New York: BasicBooks, 1978.

Redding, J. Saunders. *On Being Negro in America.* New York: Bobbs-Merrill, 1951; reprint, New York: Bantam, 1964.

———. *Stranger and Alone.* New York: Harcourt, Brace, 1950.

Reddix, Jacob L. *A Voice Crying in the Wilderness: The Memoirs of Jacob L. Reddix.* Jackson: University Press of Mississippi, 1974.

Richards, Johnetta. "The Southern Negro Youth Congress: A History." Ph.D. diss., University of Cincinnati, 1987.

Richardson, Joe M. *Christian Reconstruction: The American Missionary Association and Southern Blacks, 1861–1890.* Athens: University of Georgia Press, 1986.

———. *A History of Fisk University, 1865–1946.* Tuscaloosa: University of Alabama Press, 1980.

Robinson, Dorothy Redus. *The Bell Rings at Four: A Black Teacher's Chronicle of Change.* Austin: Madrona Press, 1978.

Robinson, Jo Ann Gibson. *The Montgomery Bus Boycott and the Women Who Started It.* Knoxville: University of Tennessee Press, 1987.

Schultz, Michael, Jr. *The National Education Association and the Black Teacher: The Integration of a Professional Association.* Coral Gables: University of Miami Press, 1970.

Shaw, Stephanie J. *What a Woman Ought to Be and to Do: Black Professional Women Workers During the Jim Crow Era.* Chicago: University of Chicago Press, 1996.

Sherer, Robert G. *Subordination or Liberation: The Development of Conflicting Theories of Education in Nineteenth-Century Alabama.* University: University of Alabama Press, 1977.

Sherrill, Josephine Price. "A Negro School-Master of the 1870s." *Journal of Negro Education* 30 (spring 1961): 163–72.

Smith, Gerald N. *A Black Educator in the Segregated South: Kentucky's Rufus B. Atwood.* Lexington: University Press of Kentucky, 1994.

Sowell, Thomas. *Assumption Versus History: Collected Papers.* Stanford CA: Hoover Institution Press, 1986.

Spivey, Donald. *Schooling for the New Slavery: Black Industrial Education, 1868–1915.* Westport CT: Greenwood Press, 1978.

Stanfield, John H. *Philanthropy and Jim Crow in American Social Science.* Westport CT: Greenwood Press, 1985.

Thornbrough, Emma Lou. "Booker T. Washington as Seen by his White Contemporaries." *Journal of Negro History* 53 (April 1968): 161–82.

Tushnet, Mark V. *The NAACP's Legal Strategy Against Segregated Education, 1925–1950.* Chapel Hill: University of North Carolina Press, 1987.

U.S. Department of Commerce, Bureau of the Census. *The Social and Economic Characteristics of the Black Population in the United States: An Historical View, 1789–1978.* Washington DC: Government Printing Office, 1978.

Vaughan, William Preston. *Schools for All: The Blacks and Public Education in the South, 1865–1877.* Lexington: University Press of Kentucky, 1977.

Walker, Vanessa Siddle. *Their Highest Potential: An African American School Community in the Segregated South.* Chapel Hill: University of North Carolina Press, 1996.

Warlick, Kenneth R. "Practical Education and the Negro College in North Carolina, 1880–1930." Ph.D. diss., University of North Carolina, 1980.

Washburne, Carleton. *A Summary Report of the Louisiana Educational Survey Commission.* Baton Rouge: Louisiana Educational Survey Commission, 1942.

Washington, Booker T. *Up From Slavery.* 1901. Reprint, New York: Norton, 1996.

Webber, Thomas L. *Deep Like the Rivers: Education in the Slave Quarters, 1831–1865.* New York: Norton, 1978.

Wheeler, Elizabeth L. "Isaac Fisher: The Frustrations of a Negro Educator at Branch Normal College, 1902–1911." *Arkansas Historical Quarterly* 41 (spring 1982): 3–50.

White, Deborah Gray. *Too Heavy a Load: Black Women in Defense of Themselves, 1894–1994.* New York: Norton, 1999.

White, Walter. *A Man Called White: The Autobiography of Walter White.* London: Victor Gollancz, 1949.

———. "Some Tactics Which Should Supplement Resort to the Courts in Achieving Racial Integration in Education." *Journal of Negro Education* 21 (winter 1952): 340–49.

Williams, Cecil J. *Freedom and Justice: Four Decades of the Civil Rights Struggle as Seen by a Black Photographer of the Deep South.* Macon: Mercer University Press, 1995.

Williams, Roger M. *The Bonds: An American Family.* New York: Atheneum, 1972.

Williams, W. T. B. "Is Tuskegee Just Another College?" *Journal of Educational Sociology* 7 (1933): 170–74.

Williamson, Joel. *New People: Miscegenation and Mulattoes in the United States.* New York: Free Press, 1980.

Wolters, Raymond. *The New Negro on Campus: Black Campus Rebellions of the 1920s.* Princeton: Princeton University Press, 1975.

Woolfolk, George R. *Prairie View: A Study in Public Conscience, 1878–1946.* New York: Pageant Press, 1962.

Wright, Richard R., Jr. *Eighty-seven Years Behind the Black Curtain: An Autobiography.* Philadelphia: Rare Book Co., 1965.

Young, Andrew J. *An Easy Burden: The Civil Rights Movement and the Transformation of America.* New York: HarperCollins, 1996.

Index